Penguin B

# GWEN HARWOOD
Selected Poems

**Gwen Harwood**, one of the most celebrated voices in Australian poetry, was born in 1920 in Brisbane, where she trained as a pianist and organist. After her marriage in 1945 she moved to Hobart, where she lived until her death in December 1995. Her first volume, *Poems*, was published in 1963; *Poems Volume II* in 1968; *The Lion's Bride* in 1981; the award-winning *Bone Scan* in 1998, and *The Present Tense* in 1995. Her numerous awards included the Grace Leven prize, the Robert Frost award, the Patrick White award, two Premier's awards and the Cholmondeley prize. She became an Officer of the Order of Australia in 1989, and was awarded several honorary doctorates.

Gwen Harwood was Australia's most distinguished librettist, best known for her collaboration over many years with Larry Sitsky.

**Gregory Kratzmann** is a Senior Lecturer in English at La Trobe University, where he teaches medieval and modern literature. He is the editor of Gwen Harwood's *Selected Letters 1943–1995*, and co-editor (with Alison Hoddinott) of a forthcoming edition of Gwen Harwood's collected poems.

# GWEN HARWOOD

### Selected Poems

Edited by Gregory Kratzmann

Penguin Books

PENGUIN BOOKS

Published by the Penguin Group
Penguin Group (Australia)
250 Camberwell Road, Camberwell, Victoria 3124, Australia
(a division of Pearson Australia Group Pty Ltd)
Penguin Group (USA) Inc.
375 Hudson Street, New York, New York 10014, USA
Penguin Group (Canada)
10 Alcorn Avenue, Toronto, Ontario, Canada M4V 3B2
(a division of Pearson Canada Inc.)
Penguin Books Ltd
80 Strand, London WC2R 0RL, England
Penguin Ireland
25 St Stephen's Green, Dublin 2, Ireland
(a division of Penguin Books Ltd)
Penguin Books India Pvt Ltd
11, Community Centre, Panchsheel Park, New Delhi – 110 017, India
Penguin Group (NZ)
Cnr Airborne and Rosedale Roads, Albany, Auckland, New Zealand
(a division of Pearson New Zealand Ltd)
Penguin Group (South Africa) (Pty) Ltd
24 Sturdee Avenue, Rosebank, Johannesburg 2196, South Africa

Penguin Books Ltd, Registered Offices: 80 Strand, London, WC2R 0RL, England

First published by Halcyon Press 2001
This edition published by Penguin Books Australia 2001

5 7 9 10 8 6

Copyright © John Harwood 2001

The moral right of the author has been asserted

All rights reserved. Without limiting the rights under copyright
reserved above, no part of this publication may be reproduced, stored
in or introduced into a retrieval system, or transmitted, in any
form or by any means (electronic, mechanical, photocopying,
recording or otherwise), without the prior written permission of both
the copyright owner and the above publisher of this book.

Cover design by Marina Messiha, Penguin Design Studio
Typeset in 11/13pt Times New Roman by Post Pre-press Group, Brisbane, Queensland
Printed and bound in Australia by McPherson's Printing Group, Maryborough, Victoria

National Library of Australia
Cataloguing-in-Publication data:

Harwood, Gwen, 1920–1995.
Selected poems

ISBN 0 14 100668 4.

I. Kratzmann, Gregory, 1949– . II. Title

A821.3

www.penguin.com.au

*To Thomas Riddell*

Grateful acknowledgement is made to the numerous journals in which these poems first appeared.

*A note on the text*

This revised and expanded selection of Gwen Harwood's poems, including poems from her last collection, *The Present Tense* (1995), was first published in this form by Halcyon Press in January 2001. The texts chosen for this edition are taken from the archive of the *Collected Poems,* which Alison Hoddinott and I have prepared for publication. In some cases we have reverted to the original journal publication (as for 'Burning Sappho' and 'Variations on a Theme') in the belief that these provide stronger readings. Occasionally, texts have been emended to reflect changes that Gwen Harwood made in her letters to friends and fellow poets, and one or two titles have been expanded in the interests of clarity.

Gwen Harwood, as is now well known, published under several other names in the 1960s and early 1970s. The poems she published as Walter Lehmann, Francis Geyer and Miriam Stone were silently reclaimed when the first edition of *Selected Poems* appeared in 1975. For this selection, I have reinstated the names under which these poems first appeared. Gwen Harwood's last *alter ego*, the youthful Hobart beat poet Timothy ('T.F.') Kline, also reappears in this edition, which concludes with a selection of 'uncollected' poems, some of which have not been published before.

I am grateful to John Harwood for inviting me to prepare this new selection. My friends and colleagues have, as always, given support and advice; in particular I would like to thank Richard Freadman, Kevin Hart, Paul Salzman and Stephanie Trigg. My greatest obligation is to Alison Hoddinott, for her generosity and discernment as an editor and critic.

*Gregory Kratzmann*

# CONTENTS

from *Poems* (1963)

| | |
|---|---|
| *Alter Ego* | 3 |
| The Wine is Drunk | 4 |
| In Hospital | 5 |
| At the Water's Edge | 6 |
| Anniversary | 7 |
| The Old Wife's Tale | 8 |
| The Glass Jar | 10 |
| A Postcard | 12 |
| *Clair de Lune* | 14 |
| *Memento Homo Quia Pulvis Es* | 15 |
| Daphne Restored | 16 |
| In Zurich by the Tideless Lake | 17 |
| "I am the Captain of My Soul" | 18 |
| *Caro Autem Infirma* | 20 |
| *Triste, Triste* | 21 |
| Home of Mercy | 22 |
| In the Park | 23 |
| At the Sea's Edge | 23 |
| O Could One Write As One Makes Love | 25 |

***Professor Eisenbart***

| | |
|---|---|
| Prize-Giving | 29 |
| Early Light | 30 |
| Professor Eisenbart's Evening | 31 |
| Daybreak | 33 |
| Panther and Peacock | 34 |
| Boundary Conditions | 36 |
| Ganymede | 37 |
| Group from Tartarus | 39 |

## from *Poems Volume Two* (1968)

| | |
|---|---|
| Nightfall | 43 |
| At the Arts Club | 44 |
| Monday | 45 |
| Afternoon | 47 |
| Hospital Evening | 48 |
| Fever | 49 |
| Ebb-tide | 51 |
| Academic Evening | 53 |
| Flying Goddess | 54 |
| Burning Sappho | 57 |
| Suburban Sonnet | 58 |
| Chance Meeting | 59 |
| Nightfall: *To the memory of Vera Cottew* | 60 |
| Four Impromptus | 62 |
| In Brisbane | 65 |
| Estuary | 67 |
| Past and Present | 68 |
| To Another Poet | 71 |
| Littoral | 72 |
| Alla Siciliana | 74 |
| Variations on a Theme | 75 |
| New Music | 79 |

## *Poems 1969–1974* from *Selected Poems* (1975)

| | |
|---|---|
| Dust to Dust | 83 |
| An Impromptu for Ann Jennings | 84 |
| Matinee | 86 |
| Reed Voices | 88 |
| Winter Quarters | 89 |
| The Violets | 91 |
| Iris | 92 |
| The Flight of the Bumble Bee | 93 |
| Night Flight | 95 |

| | |
|---|---|
| At Mornington | 98 |
| David's Harp | 100 |
| Carnal Knowledge I | 102 |
| Carnal Knowledge II | 103 |
| Night Thoughts: Baby & Demon | 104 |
| Meditation on Wyatt I | 107 |
| Meditation on Wyatt II | 108 |
| Fido's Paw Is Bleeding | 109 |
| "Thought Is Surrounded by a Halo" | 110 |
| Father and Child | 111 |
|   I  *Barn Owl* | |
|   II  *Nightfall* | |

## from *The Lion's Bride* (1981)

| | |
|---|---|
| The Lion's Bride | 117 |
| Dialogue | 117 |
| The Silver Swan | 119 |
| A Scattering of Ashes | 121 |
| A Music Lesson | 124 |
| Oyster Cove Pastorals | 126 |
|   I  *To the Muse* | |
|   II  *High Noon* | |
|   III  *Evening: "Et in Arcadia ego"* | |
| Wittgenstein and Engelmann | 129 |
| A Valediction | 132 |
| A Morning Air | 133 |
| A Little Night Music | 134 |
| The Sea Anemones | 135 |
| Death Has No Features of His Own | 136 |
| Beyond Metaphor | 136 |
| Andante | 137 |
| Seven Philosophical Poems | 138 |
|   I  *Ephemeron* | |
|   II  *Being in the World* | |

   III   *Burning the Radiata*
   IV   *Religious Instruction*
   V   *A Dream*
   VI   *A Dream of Wittgenstein*
   VII   *Some Thoughts in the 727*

| | |
|---|---:|
| The Wasps | 142 |
| Springtime, Oyster Cove | 145 |
| Evening, Oyster Cove | 146 |
| A Memory of James McAuley | 148 |
| "Let Sappho Have the Singing Head" | 149 |

   I   *Evensong*
   II   *The Head Sings, to a Guitar*
   III   *Diotima*

| | |
|---|---:|
| Mappings of the Plane | 152 |
| Return of the Native | 155 |
| The Sharpness of Death | 157 |
| Three Poems for Margaret Diesendorf | 160 |

   I   *Sparrows*
   II   *Towards a Meeting*
   III   *Memento*

A Quartet for Dorothy Hewett   163

   I   *Twilight*
   II   *Goose-girl*
   III   *A Simple Story*
   IV   *Dorothy, Reading in Hobart*

| | |
|---|---:|
| The Secret Life of Frogs | 167 |
| Space of a Dream | 169 |
| Mother Who Gave Me Life | 170 |

from ***Bone Scan*** (1988)

Class of 1927   175
  *Slate*
  *The Spelling Prize*
  *Religious Instruction*
  *The Twins*

| | |
|---|---|
| Bone Scan | 183 |
| The Night Watch | 183 |
| *I.M*. Philip Larkin | 185 |
| Divertimento | 186 |

  I  *Notturno*
  II  *Affetuoso*
  III  *Scherzo*
  IV  *Postlude: Listening to Bach*

| | |
|---|---|
| Visitor | 190 |
| Driving Home | 191 |
| The Sun Descending | 193 |
| Crow-Call | 194 |
| Sheba | 195 |
| A Feline Requiem | 196 |
| Schrödinger's Cat Preaches to the Mice | 197 |
| Litany | 198 |
| Night and Dreams | 201 |
| The Magic Land of Music | 206 |
| 1945 | 207 |
| Forty Years On | 208 |
| Sunset, Oyster Cove | 210 |
| Resurrection | 211 |
| Mid-Channel | 213 |
| Pastorals | 215 |

  I  *Threshold*
  II  *A Welcome: Flowers and Fowls*
  III  *Mt Mangana in the Distance*
  IV  *Arcady*
  V  *Reflections*
  VI  *Autumn Rain*
  VII  *Winter Afternoon*
  VIII  *Sea Eagle*
  IX  *Carapace*

from ***The Present Tense*** (1995)

| | |
|---|---|
| The Present Tense | 227 |
| Autumn | 229 |
| Midwinter Rainbow | 231 |
| Night Thoughts | 232 |
| To Music | 233 |
| Herongate | 234 |
| Wittgenstein's Shoebox | 236 |
| Songs of Eve II | 237 |
| A Piece of Ivory | 238 |
| Later Texts | 240 |
| The Owl and the Pussycat Baudelaire Rock | 242 |

## A Selection of Uncollected Poems, 1944–1994

*As Gwendoline Foster*
| | |
|---|---|
| The Rite of Spring | 245 |

*As T.F. Kline*
| | |
|---|---|
| Space Poem | 246 |
| Frog Prince | 247 |
| Emporium | 248 |

*As Gwen Harwood*
| | |
|---|---|
| Last Meeting | 249 |
| The Double Image | 250 |
| Hyacinth | 252 |
| In Memoriam Sela Trau | 254 |
| Late Works | 255 |

from *Poems* (1963)

## *Alter Ego*

Who stands beside me still,
nameless, indifferent
to any lost or ill
motion of mind or will,
whose pulse is mine, who goes
sleepless and is not spent?

Mozart said he could hear
a symphony complete,
its changing harmonies clear
plain in his inward ear
in time without extent.
And this one, whom I greet

yet cannot name, or see
save as light's sidelong shift,
who will not answer me,
knows what I was, will be,
and all I am: beyond
time's desolating drift.

In half-light I rehearse
Mozart's cascading thirds.
Light's lingering tones disperse.
Music and thought reverse
their flow. Beside dark roots
dry crickets call like birds

that morning when I came
from childhood's steady air
to love, like a blown flame,
and learned: time will reclaim
all music manifest.
Wait, then, beside my chair

as time and music flow
nightward again. I trace
their questioning voices, know
little, but learn, and go
on paths of love and pain
to meet you, face to face.

# The Wine is Drunk

The wine is drunk, the woman known.
Someone in generous darkness dries
unmanly tears for what's not found
in flesh, or anywhere. He lies
beside his love, and still alone.

Pride is a lie. His finger follows
eye, nostril, outline of the cheek.
Mortal fatigue has humbled his
exulting flesh, and all he'd seek
in a loved body's gulfs and hollows

changes to otherness: he'll never
ravish the secret of its grace.

> I must be absent from myself
> must learn to praise love's waking face,
> raise this unleavened heart, and sever
>
> from my true life this ignorant sorrow.
> I must in this gross darkness cherish
> more than all plenitude the hunger
> that drives the spirit. Flesh must perish
> yet still, tomorrow and tomorrow,

be faithful to the last, an old
blind dog that knows the stairs, and stays
obedient as it climbs and suffers.
My love, the light we'll wake to praise
beats darkness to a dust of gold.


# In Hospital

Morning. I dare not stir
for what may wake, for what pain may wake.
My daughter yesterday
unwillingly for my sake
brought here, carried with her
this jar full of odd things,
stones, shells, glass, scavengings
from our last holiday:

sea-toys, child's jewels, rolled
to smooth anonymous shapes. She filled
the jar with water to bring
a gleam back from their chilled
and speechless world. They hold
salt air, soft stone, clear light
and a swallow's ragged flight,
wings closed, continuing

in air between wave and wave.
Arrogant on that shore I raced
with my child. Pain splinters me.
I am cracked like glass. I taste
salt, my own fear, can save
nothing, am ground, degraded
on my own fragments, abraded
featureless. And am free

of pain for a brief space.
A fire-talented tongue will choose
its truth. I do not bear
what's gone, do not refuse
what's yet to come. The grace
of water rinsed, re-made
these stones. My tongue's betrayed
by pain. They speak my prayer.


# At the Water's Edge

*To Vivian Smith*

Smooth, reptilian, soaring,
a gull wheels away from this rock
leaving the scraps I was throwing,

and settles again in a flurry
of foam and plumed air. The wild seaweed
crawls crimson and green in my shadow.

The gull's flight aches in my shoulders.
It will suffer no change, cannot offer
itself to be changed, cannot suffer:

the forms born of earth are supported
by earth, body-sheltering, guileless.
"What is truth?" asks the heart, and is told:

> You will suffer, and gaze at the fact
> of the world until pain's after-image
> is as real as pain, all your strength

will be fretted to grains of distress;
you will speak to the world; what you offer
will toss upon evil and good

to be snatched or disdained. You will find
all nature exhausted as beauty
though radiant as mystery still.

You will learn what was breathed into dust
the sixth day, when the fowls of the air
wheeled over your flightless dominion.

"What is truth?" cries the heart, as the gull
rocks in changeless estate, and I turn
to my kingdom of sorrowing change.


# Anniversary

So the light falls, and so it fell
on branches leaved with flocking birds.
Light stole a city's weight to swell
the coloured life of stone. Your words
hung weightless in my ear: *Remember me.*

All words except those words were drowned
in the fresh babbling rush of spring.
In summer's dream-filled light one sound
echoed through all the whispering
galleries of green: *Remember me.*

Rods of light point home the flocking
starlings to wintry trees, and turn
stone into golden ochre, locking
the orbit of my pain. I learn
the weight of light and stone. Remember me.


# The Old Wife's Tale

Summer, transpose your haunting themes
into a key that all can sing.
How soon will winter's gadfly air
dart through the empty streets to sting
those dancers from the crowded square,
to spear their hopes and spike their dreams.


When I was young I danced so long
the fireworks stars wheeled round and burst
and showered their fierce chromatic rain
about my feet so long rehearsed
in dancing that I felt no pain
but far outdanced the dancing throng


until, beside a glass, I turned
to fix my hair and smooth my lace.
Then terror had me by the throat —
a vacant, crazed old woman's face
stared from my own. One vibrant note
cracked folly's bowl. The music burned


one moment, then its prism tones
fused into silence. Dazed and halt
I called on Christ, kind nurse, to wean

my foolish lips from sweet to salt,
erase in mercy what had been,
and melt with ease my tortured bones.

Silence for answer. So I caught
a young man's hand. He smiled and said,
"God's old and foolish, we can steal
more than our share of heavenly bread.
Rest in my arms, and I'll reveal
in darkness the true mode of thought."

I bit the core of pain, to find
this world's true sweetness on my lips,
the virtuoso senses priced
at nothing, in one vast eclipse.
A moving fingertip sufficed
to draw love's orbit through the mind.

Better than love, what name for this:
our vanished childhood sealed in flesh,
the restless energy of joy
whipping a world still morning-fresh
to hum new notes, a spinning toy.
All sorrow mended in a kiss.

My children grew. Like wine I poured
knowledge and skill, fought love's long war
with trivial cares. My spirit gave
a cry of hunger: "Grant me more
than this bare sustenance, I crave
some combat worthy of my sword."

Powerless to temper or withhold
time's raining blows, I watched him break
my cherished moulds and shape his own,
give strangers back for children, take

my husband, and I stood alone,
a shepherd with an empty fold.

Now with divining age I seek
the hidden seminal springs of peace,
hold mercy's spiral to my ear,
or stand in silence and release
the falcon mind to hunt down fear.
I stare at clouds until they break

in paradigms of truth, and spell
my sentence at the sun's assize.
My bone-bare, stark endurance frames
terror for fools, but to the wise
my winter-landscape face proclaims
life's last, and death's first parable.


# The Glass Jar

*To Vivian Smith*

A child one summer's evening soaked
a glass jar in the reeling sun
hoping to keep, when day was done
and all the sun's disciples cloaked
in dream and darkness from his passion fled,
this host, this pulse of light beside his bed.

Wrapped in a scarf his monstrance stood
ready to bless, to exorcize
monsters that whispering would rise
nightly from the intricate wood
that ringed his bed, to light with total power
the holy commonplace of field and flower.

He slept. His sidelong violence summoned
fiends whose mosaic vision saw
his heart entire. Pincer and claw,
trident and vampire fang, envenomed
with his most secret hate, reached and came near
to pierce him in the thicket of his fear.

He woke, recalled his jar of light,
and trembling reached one hand to grope
the mantling scarf away. Then hope
fell headlong from its eagle height.
Through the dark house he ran, sobbing his loss,
to the last clearing that he dared not cross:

the bedroom where his comforter
lay in his rival's fast embrace
and faithless would not turn her face
from the gross violence done to her.
Love's proud executants played from a score
no child could read or realize. Once more

to bed, and to worse dreams he went.
A ring of skeletons compelled
his steps with theirs. His father held
fiddle and bow, and scraped assent
to the malignant ballet. The child dreamed
this dance perpetual, and waking screamed

fresh morning to his window-sill.
As ravening birds began their song
the resurrected sun, whose long
triumph through flower-brushed fields would fill
night's gulfs and hungers, came to wink and laugh
in a glass jar beside a crumpled scarf.

# A Postcard

Snow crusts the boughs' austere entanglement.
Bare spines once fleshed in summer's green delights
pattern an ice-green sky. Three huntsmen go
vested for the ritual of the hunt
with lean, anonymous dogs for acolytes.
Shadowless, luminous, their world of snow
superlative in paint: so we assume
on snowlit air mortality's faint plume.

Often in the museum I would stand
before this picture, while my father bent
to teach me its perfections. It became
part of the love that leapt from hand to hand
in a live current; a mind-made continent
familiar as my shadow or my name
were the near, sprawling arabesque of thorns,
the looping skaters, and the towering horns

the Moses-mountain lifted, gripping its stone
covenant between cold and solitude.
My four-square world! Homesickness, sit in tears
turning the mind's old scrapbook, the long known
pastiche of yesterdays, believing good
and incorruptible the uneasy years
of childhood learning treachery in its slow
budding of cells, and heartsblood on the snow

that day my dolls did not return my kiss.
In their blank eyes all flashing evidence
sank to lack-lustre glass; about me spilled
the shrouding light of a new genesis.
No hand lay palm to mine in innocence.
A blind, beaked hunger, crying to be filled,

nestled and gaped, was fed, and whipped again
in bird-clear syllables of mortal pain

through a rare kingdom crumbling into paint.
A father's magus mantle sleeved no longer
an old man's trembling gestures towards his gift
sealed in with myrrh; and sovereign youth grew faint
hearing that crystal voice cry still the hunger
tented in flesh: "Time's herod-blade is swift.
Hunt me down love, the snow-white unicorn,
I'll drink in safety from its twisted horn

your childhood's relic poison, and lie quiet."
Now I am old. The fabulous beast, grown tame,
dreams in heraldic stillness of the chase;
the sick heart, chafed by memory's salt-rough diet,
craves for lost childish sweetness, cannot name
its old heroic themes. My early face
withered to bone, fretted by wintry change,
flowering in blood-bright cheek and lip grows strange:

my children's children, with my father's eyes
stare with me at this postcard, seeing only
a sharp and simple winter, while they wear
the hard sun like a skin. And my love lies
imprisoned in stiff gestures, hearing the lonely
voice call "I hunger" through the snow-bright air.
Spilling the days no memory will restore
time's fountain climbs its own perpetual core.

# *Clair de Lune*

*Poet to Bluestocking*

Let us walk with this cone of light
lying seaward. It points where earth's ashen
impoverished fragment importunes
all oceans and lovers and poets,
whose waxing has made and whose waning
unmade you, whose wall-scaling tinsel
has captured your vizored city.

On our right lie flickering houses
but seaward emptiness filters through
your inhaling nostrils. You nibble at space,
blot a starfield out with a starfish hand,
while streaking and scraping the moonlit shore
your image deformed scrawls a body
impenetrable by this light.

As tensile as spider webbing
is your nightshade self, is your weightless
unliving siege in this scandalous town.
In Amazon forests the Indians
empty the stomachs of captured apes
and parrots that feed in unscalable trees,
then feed on the half-digested fruits.

So towering spirits caught
by your prick-eared wit are opened
and an after-image of rapture, a fragment of passion
savoured and sucked.
                    Ah, nature
is wasteful, the wild thrust of lovers
is careless, the flux of this swarming sea
is endless. The artist alone

is sparing. In light from a single source,
with calm and indolent judgment,
with the tip of a pen, with a paintbrush,
he will seal and transfigure the changing face
of truth, which is living, and moving with us as we walk,
and stays with the lovers who lie in creation's act:
like this cone of light on the sea.


## *Memento Homo Quia Pulvis Es*
—Genesis iii. 19

Policeman postman watchman fireman
airman madman bird man rubbish man
mothers and their gingerbread men
children snowmen
                       gone are gone.
Dust without dimension swallows
rain and wind and rioting sun.
The seas' dense mantle arches, hollows,
sinks, forms again on monstrous tides.
The last of life: a sack of scars
trapped in death's whirlpool, shudders, claws
light's grey suffusion, till dust hides
its freakish agony.
                       Galaxies
on fire with irony collide
praising with light their final cause.

# Daphne Restored

*Also vor allem das Schwersein*
—Rilke

Never will flesh and bone ascend
in myriad-green significance,
never with bird or raindrop dance
light-veined on shifting planes of wind.

Words whispering among my boughs
from lovers in the moving shade
who unrehearsed in sorrow made
their time-annihilating vows

or turned in mutual warmth to pluck
love's classic fruit, entwined a wreath
of hope blown on the flute of breath.
I slept, until the lightning struck.

Bones in a twisting prism of fire,
whipcord sinew, shuddering nerves
fused with flesh in tender curves.
Deep within the central spire

muscled and globed, a pulse began.
Filmy membranes cleared to find
entire, embraced by weightless mind
the rhymed anatomy of man

freed from a charred concavity
to learn the authentic modes of breath,
sleep's intimate mimicry of death;
to know, when morning from the eye

scours visions of invading fire
and tighter draws light's thread to suture
waking to waking grief, the future
measure of tears, and still aspire

above the body's weight, its urn
of unproliferating bones,
to heights where fading overtones
of fire and molten alloys burn,

still hope in love's brief peace to drown
the whispering of the sleepless mind
that frames all words and cannot find
one word to call the lightning down.


# In Zurich by the Tideless Lake

In Zurich by the tideless lake
a sculptured Ganymede extends
one hand to heaven, one to a god-
proud eagle.
               Blind, one's hand might take
the course of bronze as those legs break
apart to bear the metal's weight.

Once in a shadowless time we lived
as gods might live, took light from fire
and fire from light, in wholeness thrived
on blinding rapture as we sieved
light's charity through celebrant hands.

Blind, one might hear a whistling boy.

With ravening beak and talons tense
for mastery the spirit drops
from its inhuman height on sense
clouding with anguish. But the body
with darkness for its evidence
discerns no god, though in its gathering
nightfall from living tissue shine
godheads of light and fire assumed
from our love's light and bodies' fire.
Darkness clouds your eyes, or mine —
no matter whose, when each will suffer
gross darkness for the other's sake.

A bronze boy whistles by the lake.


## "I am the Captain of My Soul"

*The human body is the best picture of the human soul*
—Ludwig Wittgenstein

But the Captain is drunk, and the crew
hauling hard on his windlass of fury are whipped
by his know-nothing rage. Their terror
troubles the sunlight. "Now tell me,"
the Captain says, as his drunkenness
drifts into tears, "what's to keep me
at ease in this harbour?"
                        "We'll tell you,"
say Hands, "in our headlong chase through a fugue

for three voices, you heard a fourth voice naming
divisions of silence. We'll summon
that voice once again, it may tell you

of marvels wrung from sorrow endured."
"We have seen," say Eyes, "how in Venice
the steps of churches open and close
like marble fans under water."

"You can rot in your sockets," the Captain cries.

"I have children," says Body, haloed
in tenderness, firm in ripeness still.
"I grew gross with their stress, I went spinning
in a vortex of pain. I gave my breast
and its beauty to nourish their heedless growth.
They jump on my shadow in mischievous joy.
On their lives your astonishing sorrows
flow easy as water on marble steps."

*"Lass sie betteln gehn!"* roars the Captain
as his old wounds burn, and he gulps
from his flagon of grief. "You servants, you things,
stand up there! *You* with the ageing choir-boy face,
and *you* with your facile dexterity, *you*
with your marble hallucinations, COME!"

Hands, eyes, body keel to the void as the drunken
Captain sings in his wilderness of water.

## *Caro Autem Infirma*

Often I wake in darkness
from a dream to a crying bird or child
and hear faint cockcrows summon
a time unreconciled
with sleep or waking.
Who turns by the heart's brazier
untempered eyes on the common
denials of nightmare shielding
the sleeper from worse waking?

I walked on water. Night's hollow
cranium sutured by lightning globed
miraculous visions. A flame-like
hand drew the waters robed
in tempest to naked
calm. The black deep sustained me
and past and future came like
the arms of a cross to hold me
fast in time's flux, rejoicing.

I grappled that night the protean
inscape of self, and held it fast
one moment, prophesying
in its true shape at last
my inward epic:
life's flowering *now* enclosing
its bitterest fruit, a dying
brazier, and fugitive cockcrows
in cadence on cadence enshrouding

the fossils of youth (ah, Renoir-
flesh!) Light's twittering servants shrill
good news of their lord's returning,
his night-rinsed winecups fill
between cypress and cypress
as children wake to his goldsmith-
graining, his radiance burning
dreams' spade-black mischief from bodies
that walk on day's flood, rejoicing.


## *Triste, Triste*

In the space between love and sleep
when heart mourns in its prison
eyes against shoulder keep
their blood-black curtains tight.
Body rolls back like a stone, and risen
spirit walks to Easter light;

away from its tomb of bone,
away from the guardian tents
of eyesight, walking alone
to unbearable light with angelic
gestures. The fallen instruments
of its passion lie in the relic

darkness of sleep and love.
And heart from its prison cries
to the spirit walking above:
"I was with you in agony.
Remember your promise of paradise,"
and hammers and hammers, "Remember me."

So the loved other is held
for mortal comfort, and taken,
and the spirit's light dispelled
as it falls from its dream to the deep
to harrow heart's prison so heart may waken
to peace in the paradise of sleep.

*Walter Lehmann*


# Home of Mercy

By two and two the ruined girls are walking
at the neat margin of the convent grass
into the chapel, counted as they pass
by an old nun who silences their talking.

They smooth with roughened hands the clumsy dress
that hides their ripening bodies. Memories burn
like incense as towards plaster saints they turn
faces of mischievous children in distress.

They kneel: time for the spirit to begin
with prayer its sad recourse to dream and flight
from their intolerable weekday rigour.
Each morning they will launder, for their sin,
sheets soiled by other bodies, and at night
angels will wrestle them with brutish vigour.

*Walter Lehmann*

# In the Park

She sits in the park. Her clothes are out of date.
Two children whine and bicker, tug her skirt.
A third draws aimless patterns in the dirt.
Someone she loved once passes by — too late

to feign indifference to that casual nod.
"How nice," *et cetera*. "Time holds great surprises."
From his neat head unquestionably rises
a small balloon ... "but for the grace of God ...."

They stand awhile in flickering light, rehearsing
the children's names and birthdays. "It's so sweet
to hear their chatter, watch them grow and thrive,"
she says to his departing smile. Then, nursing
the youngest child, sits staring at her feet.
To the wind she says, "They have eaten me alive."

*Walter Lehmann*


# At the Sea's Edge

Sea at this town's neat threshold spills its gloss
of cold, of distance. Urban colours toss

in thousand-faceted water. Gulls outrace
the wavering wind. A crowd comes to this place

daily, gathers to watch a tame seal fed.
They smile to see its grave grey-whiskered head

cruise by the fish-punt, its dense body dive
with ecstasy of balance through its live

element for scraps. A car stops. One by one
three people step into the lavish sun.

The crowd stirs, looks, and looks away to find
darkness upon the water: one is blind.

And worse than blind; as in a hideous mask
degraded eyelids squint. Young children ask,

"What —?" and are hushed, as the blind woman stands
between a man and woman, with her hands

held gently; neither proud nor humble turns
her ruined face to the oblique wind and learns

what the blind learn from wind. Beyond her night
green beards of seaweed drip, light, light, light, light,

where water sucks and shudders round half-rotten
staves of the wharf, and murmurs long forgotten

furies of wave on rock. Of light no trace
of recollection marks her ravaged face,

only the sea-wind speaks to her. The crowd
melts, lest ill-luck should touch them. A torn cloud

of gulls descends, disputing scraps. The sea
is marked by the wind's tread, that may not be

told or foreseen, but wanders where it will,
speaking its comfort to the spirit still

in darkness. "Look," says the man, "he begs! He shakes
his whiskers like a dog." Green water flakes

in silver from the seal. The woman cries
"Look! Now he's diving. Look, he's got his eyes

right on that scrap of fish. He never misses!
He goes like a torpedo." Water hisses

and churns in the seal's wake. As the three stand
silent, the blind one smiles. From hand to hand

a live hope flows. The wind walks on the sea,
printing the water's face with charity.

*Walter Lehmann*


# O Could One Write As One Makes Love

O could one write as one makes love
when all is given and nothing kept,
then language might put by at last
its coy elisions and inept
withdrawals, yield, and yielding cast
aside like useless clothes the crust
of worn and shabby use, and trust
its candour to the urgent mind,
its beauty to the searching tongue.
Safe in the world's great house with all
its loves and griefs, at ease among
its earthly fruits, original
as earth and air, the body learns
peace, while the mind in torment burns

to strip the cloak of daily use
from language. Could one seize and move
the stubborn words to yield and sing, —like Herbert —difficulty
then one would write as one makes love
and poems and revelations spring
like children from the mind's desire,
original as light and fire.

*Walter Lehmann*

**Professor Eisenbart**

# Prize-Giving

Professor Eisenbart, asked to attend
a girls' school speech night as an honoured guest
and give the prizes out, rudely declined;
but from indifference agreed, when pressed
with dry scholastic jokes, to change his mind,
to grace their humble platform, and to lend

distinction (of a kind not specified)
to the occasion. Academic dress
became him, as he knew. When he appeared
the girls whirred with an insect nervousness,
the Head in humbler black flapped round and steered
her guest, superb in silk and fur, with pride

to the best seat beneath half-hearted blooms
tortured to form the school's elaborate crest.
Eisenbart scowled with violent distaste,
then recomposed his features to their best
advantage: deep in thought, with one hand placed
like Rodin's Thinker. So he watched the room's

mosaic of young heads. Blonde, black, mouse-brown
they bent for their Headmistress' opening prayer.
But underneath a light (no accident
of seating, he felt sure), with titian hair
one girl sat grinning at him, her hand bent
under her chin in mockery of his own.

Speeches were made and prizes given. He shook
indifferently a host of virgin hands.
"Music!" The girl with titian hair stood up,
hitched at a stocking, winked at near-by friends,
and stood before him to receive a cup
of silver chased with curious harps. He took

her hand, and felt its voltage fling his hold
from his calm age and power; suffered her strange
eyes, against reason dark, to take his stare
with her to the piano, there to change
her casual schoolgirl's for a master's air.
He forged his rose-hot dream as Mozart told

the fullness of all passion or despair
summoned by arrogant hands. The music ended,
Eisenbart teased his gown while others clapped,
and peered into a trophy which suspended
his image upside down: a sage fool trapped
by music in a copper net of hair.

# Early Light

Light's planet-leaping shafts go home
  at last between closed lids that keep
knowledge of day's advancing tide
  from the uneasy house of sleep.

Professor Eisenbart looks up
  to see his mistress half awake
smoothing her sleep-indented skin.
  He hears the crested minutes break

into a bleak expanse of hours,
  and through the ruined palisade
of dream-horizoned arms and thighs
  strides time with heartbreak on his blade.

A painting from the Lascaux caves
  hangs reproduced above their bed:
bird-masked beside his wounded prey
  an ithyphallic hunter dead.


## Professor Eisenbart's Evening

Two schoolboys by a bare brick wall
snigger at my approach and scrawl
crude verities in pilfered chalk.
Passion's old nicknames sear their talk,
swell hot and rankling on my tongue.
Let copulation thrive among
these tedious three-piece-cultured miles.
Suburbs, preserve your tribal styles.

Spring's catkin fingers droop to bless
my mistress' gateway, and caress
my loosening cheek. Shall I release
into this nightfall-conjured peace
my stalking Jack-the-Ripper heart?
Whom shall I shear and slice apart?
— Dearest, what did you do today?
"Slept late, as is my usual way.
Did usual things at usual hours.
Went shopping, read, arranged the flowers."
— Come, now.
             "The moon forestalls you, dear."
— One day I'll crack that pestering sphere,
that night-spy, womanish Peeping Tom.
I'll rip her with some glorious bomb.
I'll blow her to oblivion
and howl with laughter when she's gone.

There'll be no tides in women's blood.
"What torment lights this feverish mood?
I'll go to sleep, and you can lie
and calculate the root of *pi*,
work out what formulae you need,
what cobalt, hydrogen, to speed
the great bomb's liberating shock
and crack the cold-short lunar rock
and free poor men from her dominion.
It can't be done, in my opinion."

> Rest, nervous mind. Why do you stare
> through quiet streets where doubt, despair
> and all day's peevish brood have passed
> through day's long ritual at last
> to the absolving sign of sleep?
> One corner of this town I keep
> harbours a Something, scuffling, sly,
> shooting like moonlight past the eye,
> sinister, whispering half aloud,
> stirring the shadows to a cloud
> of poison-thick, inhuman ill.
> Invulnerable, and swift to kill.
>
> Rest, rest. Orion, this calm spring night,
> leaps from his unassailable height
> and through your labyrinthine town
> hunts the unquiet intruder down.

# Daybreak

The snails brush silver. Critic crow
  points his unpleasant beak, and lances.
Resumes his tree-top, darts below
  his acid-bright, corrosive glances.

In the hushed corridors of sleep
  Professor Eisenbart plots treason.
Caretaker mind prepares to sweep
  the dusty offices of reason.

Eisenbart mutters, wakes in rage
  because crow's jarring *c-a-a-r-k-s* distress him.
His mistress grins, refers to age
  and other matters which oppress him.

He scowls purse-lipped. She yawns, and throws
  her arms in scarecrow crucifixion.
Clear of the hills, light's wafer shows
  in world-without-end benediction.

She makes him tea. He sips and calms
  his Royal Academic temper,
while Life and Day outside shout psalms
  in antiphon . . . . *Et nunc et semper.*

# Panther and Peacock

Professor Eisenbart, with grim distaste,
skirted the laughter of a Sunday crowd
circling an ape's gross mimicry of man.
His mistress watched a peacock. He grimaced,
making rude observations on the proud
creature's true centre of that radiant fan.

Raked by the aureoled bird's nerve-twisting cries
they strolled away, affecting noble ease.
A clot of darkness moved in temperate shade:
a jungle climate, favouring decay,
flared through the keyholes of a panther's eyes
to tarnish the gold gauze of sun, and fade

blue from the brilliant air.
                            "Glutted with leisure
dull-coupled citizens and their buoyant young
gape at your elegant freedom, and my face
closed round the cares of power, see with mean pleasure
age scaling massive temples overhung
with silver mists of hair — that handspan space

corners their destiny: at my word they'll bear
acerebrate hybrid monsters. *Fiat nox*!
Let the dark beast whose cat-light footpads scour
my cortex barren leap from its cage and tear
their feathers out!"
                        His mistress said, "What shocks
await the bourgeois! In this twilight hour

the earth blooms velvet-soft, while its immense
authority of volume fails and dies
with the clear colours of substantial day.
Now the sharp iconography of sense

declines to vague abstraction, let your eyes
socket the blaze of Venus, through the play

of leaves in the last branch-caught stir of wings.
Rest here."
                      She cradled his Darwinian head.
Its intricate landscape of fine lines and scars,
ridges and hollows, veins' meanderings,
grew desolate in sleep. Above them spread
a leaf-divided tissue of space and stars.

He dreamed: he walked at sunset through the same
gardens; safe on his tongue the incredible
formula that, spoken, would impel
prodigious ruin. His mistress called his name.
Feathers sprang from the sutures of his skull.
His hands grew rattling quills. As darkness fell

it circumfused worse darkness, in which prowled
familiar nightmare towards him, cowering, gripped
as always fast in horror. A stale breath
of carrion choked him. Fingerless, dewlap-jowled,
bird-beaked, he screamed in silence, and was ripped
awake still rooted in his dream of death.

His mind deep in the vehemence of shade
groped worldwards. Though his body showed no harm,
stone-still, with sorrow frozen on her face
the young girl bent above him. While they made
this strange *pietà*, feathers glistening warm
with his own heartstain fell through infinite space.

# Boundary Conditions

"At the sun's incredible centre
  the atomic nuclei
with electrons and light quanta
  in a burning concord lie.
All the particles that form
  light and matter, in that furnace
keep their equilibrium.
  Once we pass beyond the surface
of the star, sharp changes come.
  These remarks apply as well
to the exploding atom bomb,"
  said Professor Eisenbart
while his mistress, with a shell
  scored an arrow and a heart
in the sand on which they lay
  watching heat and light depart
from the boundaries of day.

"Sprung from love's mysterious core
  soul and flesh," the young girl said,
"restless on the narrow shore
  between the unborn and the dead,
split from concord, and inherit
  mankind's old dichotomy:
mind and matter; flesh and spirit;
  what has been and what will be;
desire that flares beyond our fate:
  still in the heart more violence lies
than in the bomb. Who'll calculate
  that tough muscle's bursting size?"

Tongues of darkness licked the crust
  of pigment from the bowl of blue.
Thought's campaniles fell to dust
  blown by the sea-wind through and through.


## Ganymede

Springtime: the eye once, scaling alps of blossom
might have traced in curdling cloud the foolproof shine
of a god's descent, a god's claws lifting the lissom
sweetness of mortal youth from sure decline —

the Phrygian mode. Light poking past his nose
compelled Professor Eisenbart to witness
spring's lyric conquest of his room. He rose,
thought of his mistress and her tiresome sweetness,

and turning from his work to earth's green text
by flowers' sharp asterisks found himself drawn
to footnotes of unwelcome longing, vexed
to see below him on the hotel lawn

the cause of his unrest: a boy whose wealth
of beauty, gathered now beneath the tragic
green of a cypress, had seduced by stealth
since their first meeting, Eisenbart from his magic

formulae. Descending by the stairs
(he feared the lift's steel cage), passing a room
where idle women nursed their lapdog cares,
he reached the formal garden with its gloom

of cypress and tormented hedge enfolding
the boy's still-life repose. And if the women
saw them ascend the stairs, Eisenbart holding
the boy's hand in his own, it was a human

fabric that drew their sighs: youth's gold warp threading
its joy through darker woof. His rented heaven
enclosed them both at last. Eisenbart treading
the orbit of his hope felt a warm leaven

lighten his bones, nerves, arteries; expand
the burden of his breath until he choked
and tasted his own panic, shocked, unmanned:
smiling assent that could not be revoked

the boy, bred in the slippery city, stared
with childhood's cunning at a future come
too soon. His graceful ivory body, bared,
spoke of itself alone. Corruption, dumb,

winked, a sour beggar, through his perfect eyes
miming its own deceit in flesh and feature.
Eisenbart, who might upon that prize
have dropped as the hawk swoops to serve its nature,

felt, softer than snow on water or on snow,
a winter's delicate absences reclaim him.
Ganymede, with crude mockery, chose to go.
Eisenbart took his pen; let sunset frame him

a city fringed with water and cold light,
restless with growing life; and turned to live,
to work in his own world, where symbols might
speak to him their sublime affirmative.

# Group from Tartarus

A woman ripe with life, whose hand
flashed a wide wedding ring, had stopped
to greet two children not her own
who waiting for a parent hopped
bird-quick from slab to slab of stone.
Their father: and what sorrow spanned

love's light-through-eyeball race and flow
above the children's heads, what gift
this moment was from sweepstake fate
while the cloud-sliding watery drift
of winter hung above the weight
his children and her ring might show

of earlier love, no passer-by
except Professor Eisenbart
interpreted. He paused and read,
or seemed to read, the weather chart.
Still weary from his mistress' bed
he read at sight, from eye to eye,

their fugue of love and loss, and traced
the stretto of their parting words.
Lightly across the pavement slabs
a seagull walked. The sea-clean bird's
reptilian head made lightning stabs
gutterwards at some rotting waste.

Eisenbart felt, who prized his dry
indifference to love and luck,
uncharted cold that winter day
as a hard beak of anguish struck
the ripe waste of his heart's decay:
*Too old to love, too young to die.*

from *Poems Volume Two* (1968)

# Nightfall

One evening when a genial air
ruffled the jacaranda trees
Professor Kröte spread his square
musician's hands on his plump knees,
and, sighing, sat alone among the uncaring
derelict drunks, and lovers, while the flaring

coat of the river glowed and flamed
with sunset, and declined to drab
monotony, and smokestacks framed
in saffron light rose up to stab
his breast with memories: a yellow sky;
cypress, jet-black; a boy plays "Islamei"

with arrogant skill; his teacher claws
a fine gilt chair with nervous pride —
and then the turbulent applause;
rococo gods and cherubs ride
his winds of promise, and their gilded scrolls
shine in that glittering hall; the Danube rolls

past those high windows in its skin
of sunset.
      "Who would know me now,
a second-rate musician in
an ignorant town? Or tell me how
discords of fading light find and restore
the colours of a day that comes no more?"

So Kröte mused, as if his lost
hope darkened on the water's face.
The poor drunks slept beneath a host
of falling flowers. In light embrace

awaiting night, young lovers moved their tender
hands with instinctive gestures of surrender.

Sleep with its textureless draperies
curtained him. His lean spirit stayed
watchful among the shaken trees
drinking God's peace, and humbly prayed
for daily bread, for one hour when he might
rejoice, that his soul be not required that night.

Kröte, waking from troubled rest,
tossing his wild musician's hair,
feeling the torment leave his breast
and vanish in the gentle air,
knew he must find, in his soul's night, alone,
what more the city held than brick and stone.

*Francis Geyer*

# At the Arts Club

Kröte is drunk, but still can play.
Knick-knacks in shadow-boxes wink
at gewgaws while he grinds away
at Brahms, not much the worse for drink.

The hostess pats her tinted curls.
Sees, yawning surreptitiously,
a bitch in black with ginger pearls
squeezing the local tenor's knee.

Kröte lets the loud pedal blur
a dubious trill. The variations
on Handel's foursquare theme occur
to most as odd manipulations

of something better left alone.
They suffer. Kröte knows they do:
with malice adds some more, his own,
and plays all the repeats right through.

He was expected to perform
a waltz, or something short and sweet.
The coffee's made, the supper's warm,
the ravenous guests would love to eat.

Sober, Kröte's inclined to gloom.
Drunk, he becomes a sacred clown.
He puffs and pounds and shakes the room.
An ill-placed ornament falls down.

A pause. Chairs squeak. The hostess claps,
wrongly — there's still the fugue to play.
Tenor and Ginger Pearls, perhaps
for ever, boldly sneak away.

*Francis Geyer*


# Monday

Kröte sits on the beach at noon
   drinking the blood-red wine.
"Oh how shall I pluck from air some tune
   to match this life of mine?"

A Council notice close at hand
  says liquor is forbidden.
In a damp hollow in the sand
  he keeps his bottle hidden.

A few young mothers come his way.
  They frown at Kröte, jerking
their children past as if to say
  decent men would be working.

Kröte thinks: If I had a child . . .
  and dreams himself a creature
with smoky hair, whose spirit's wild
  as wind, whose inmost nature

mirrors his love. The crowding gulls
  rise, as a dumpy likeness
of Kröte's dream, in spectacles,
  stones them. A wave of sickness

shakes him. The child comes close, and hangs
  over him with a grin,
then with her metal spade she bangs
  sharply on Kröte's shin.

Kröte flinches with pain, and scowls,
  "Mädchen, why do you hit me?"
He grabs the lifted spade. She howls
  "Don't let that bad man get me."

The women turn from their affairs.
  The vicious child lets loose a
torrent of lies. Her mother glares
  at Kröte like Medusa.

"Monster! You filthy pervert!" scream
  the child-envenomed jury;
round his condemned retreat they seam
  the tissue of their fury.

In vain this night will Kröte try
  on the rinsed beach to find
his wine, or lose the thoughts that lie
  like stains upon his mind.

*Francis Geyer*


# Afternoon

Kröte has spent some time devising
a kind of storage bin for tunes.
His cupboard's full of sheets comprising
the work of drunken afternoons.

Nothing today comes of his labours.
" 'Revenge, revenge' Timotheus cries,"
bellows a hopeful bass — the neighbour's
a singing coach. As Kröte tries

to catch the semiquavers, swearing
and whistling through his snow-white teeth,
Beethoven frowns in plaster, wearing
Kröte's hat on his laurel wreath.

A pupil comes. The noise is fearful.
From next door come contralto wails.
Kröte is forced to have an earful
of Gounod with his pupil's scales.

While she fights Bach he scribbles crudely
in ink across her virgin score.
She murmurs, and he asks her rudely,
"Stupid, what do you pay me for?"

Then he sits scowling at the scowling
features of the illustrious dead.
Between the wrong notes and the howling
he must endure, and earn his bread.

*Francis Geyer*


# Hospital Evening

Sunset: the blaze of evening burns
through curtains like a firelit ghost.
Kröte, dreaming of snow, returns
to something horrible on toast

slapped at him by a sulky nurse
whose boyfriend's waiting. Kröte loves
food. Is this food? He finds it worse
than starving, as he cuts and shoves

one nauseating mouthful down.
Kröte has managed to conceal
some brandy in his dressing gown.
He gulps it fast, until the real

sunset's a field of painted light
and his white curtains frame a stage
where he's the hero and must fight
his fever. He begins to rage

fortissimo in German, flings
the empty bottle on the floor;
roars for more brandy, thumps and sings.
Three nurses crackle through the door

and hold him down. He struggles, then
submits to the indignities
nurses inflict, and sleeps again,
dreaming he goes, where the stiff trees

glitter in silence, hand in hand
with a young child he does not know,
who walking makes no footprint and
no shadow on soft-fallen snow.

*Francis Geyer*

# Fever

Kröte lies feverish and sick
in hospital where sterile gleams
of chrome pluck at his aching head.
Pain wrings his hands, a phantom double
out of control. Some fever-trick
beguiles a desolate hour: he dreams
a host of friends come to his bed
with fruit and wine. But who would trouble

to flesh the unstaged reality
of Kröte's dreams? Someone. He wakes
to see one of his pupils standing
close to him, a thin child whose plain

features, unformed as yet, could be
ugly or beautiful. She makes
no secret of her undemanding
worship, is happy to remain

awkwardly, in school uniform,
ignorant of her inmost hunger,
thinking of love as a child may —
gentle kisses and sweets. "I've brought
a gift." As Kröte takes the warm
packet, his chill hand feels a younger
quick-fingered grasp; she tears away
the wrapping. Gift. *Vergiftet*. Caught

between two languages his mind
falters. *Gift*. Poison. Fever wears
his flesh. His sickness raps upon
façades beyond which Nothing grins.
Demons and near-men howl behind
his headache, but the young girl stares
transfixed as if a great light shone
from Kröte's face. A nurse begins

her rounds: sees on his bed the box
of sweets. "You can't have those." His hands
close on the box. A ludicrous
struggle ensues as Kröte holds
harder, frowns like Beethoven, locks
fingers of power. His pupil stands
giggling, while Kröte, furious,
triumphant, glares at the nurse, who scolds

her patient as she would a child,
and, thinking that his pupil is
his daughter, leaves the two alone.
Kröte leans on his pillow, breathing

as if asleep. It seems the wild
mane of his hair is touched. A kiss
light as a wafer? Or his own
imagining? He sleeps. A seething

darkness finds where his life is laid.
Maps of an empty continent,
himself, are drawn in bleeding scrawls.
Keep me, his spirit prays, from ill.
By its own scope the heart's betrayed
to monstrous dreams, and throbs assent:
"I'll make the creature mine." He falls
through a black void, himself, and still

falling wakes into darkness, crying
"Poison!" A tired sister lays
her book aside and jabs his arm.
Rest shall be given where rest is wanted.
Elsewhere this night a child is lying
restless, sure-hearted as she prays
innocently for undreamed-of harm,
then sleeps, certain her prayer is granted.

*Francis Geyer*


# Ebb-tide

Now that you have no word for me
I bring your bitter silence here
where the tide rustles from the land
seaward, its whispered meaning clear.
My young son chases, stone in hand,
a sandcrabs' rattling greyblue army.

He stones the scuttling host, and gathers
one crippled prize. Cannot decide
which is its head. As dying claws
tickle his palm, he laughs. The tide
withdraws for his delight. We pause
at every pool. The mind surrenders

its agony to littoral creatures
rocked in the comfort of the shore's
unvarying seasons. A smooth spine
held in my idle fingers scores
a name in sand as the gulls sign
the windless water with your features.

I have one picture of you taken
picnicking somewhere: mountains, clouds
beyond a pier; incredibly blue
water surrounds you, masts and shrouds
pattern unheard-of azure. You
smile there forever. Time has shaken

life from the sea, flung on dry land
bones that got upright, fleshed their wild
sea-creature grins, and learned the weight
of earth. I run beside my child
stoning the crabs with mindless hate.
The sea withdraws from the gold sand.

*Francis Geyer*

# Academic Evening

Scandal and clever-silly talk
circulate faster. In his chair
Professor Kröte puffs and plays
as usual the gross buffoon.
A woman like a crippled hawk
sits brooding while two colleagues tear
her work to shreds. My neighbour flays
the latest book of poems. A tune

from nowhere settles in my brain.
The last guest comes. I tremble as
my pulse grows furious. Somehow
on her your ravishing likeness lies.
Straightway my resurrected pain
walks through the ruined night. She has
your look, your gestures. Turning now
she's strange again. Her voice implies

her otherness. But I'm so sharp
with loss, I see how Kröte's eyes
wait upon hers, and are rejected.
The torn bluestocking on my right
leans closer, and begins to harp
on Anglo-Saxon Homilies.
Once more our glasses are collected
and filled, and Kröte's clowning's tight

with anguish as I spin upon
the carrousel of drunkenness
that turns me through a hemisphere
from this chance likeness to your face,

your own, unmatched by anyone.
I whirl, I fly in mortal stress.
A tart voice cackles in my ear
as back I wheel into this place

where Kröte drinks and clowns his way
across his tightrope of despair,
eating queer sea-food from a stick.
Men do not weep in public places
in this land. On a tragic day
men gathered in San Marco's square:
the campanile, brick by brick,
subsided. From Italian faces

the tears streamed. Here men would not spill
tears if a campanile fell.
Yes fill my glass. That morning's gone
from time forever when I lay
naked beside my love. Yes fill
my glass until the carrousel
of drunken stars I ride upon
shall whirl me beyond night or day.

*Francis Geyer*


# Flying Goddess

Kröte plays in a salon full
of rubbish artfully arrayed.
Someone who cannot play at all
waits with assured impatience by
a cube of plastic labelled DIE
to criticize what will be played.

Kröte, hoping the drinks will last,
essays a waterfall of notes.
A waitress with a tray goes past.
He stumbles. A green leg pursued
by a disintegrating nude
hangs nearby. Round the music floats

a haze of adjectives, all snatched
from last week's art reviews: committed,
spare, dense, centripetal, detached.
Green leg forever wilt thou run
as I will when this piece is done
thinks Kröte, thirstily quickwitted.

Faint overtones of his last chord
die round his empty seat. He knows
the office where the drink is stored,
and soon, with easy triumph bearing
pilfered bottle and glass, still wearing
his Great Musician frown, he goes

to drink for a long interval
in a deserted studio.
A batik picture on the wall
springs suddenly to life: a Flying
Goddess made luminous by dying
sunlight. In a last western glow

her gold-edged feet and fingers shine.
In labyrinthine fantasies
her scarf weaves rapid arcs of line
blue round her skin of ebony.
A gold and scarlet fluency
of dress enfolds her slender thighs.

"Goddess, dear lady," Kröte says,
"wait in the glow and dazzle of
your high transparent distances!"
He smiles, and drinks himself a new
environment of airy blue.
Weightless in space he soars above

the solid foreigner whose face
between one vision and the next
is Kröte's, to his native place
in gentle, all-sustaining air,
far from his sober prison where
an unintelligible text

is thrust at him, beyond the sneers
of those who talk, but can't perform.
Night falls. The gilding disappears
from his sublime, immortal friend.
Day and his bottle reach their end.
"Goddess," he says, "you have the charm

of all that flows, yet still you stay
unmoving in your classic sky.
Bless me!" He picks a drunken way
through the dark salon, feeling sick;
yet pauses long enough to kick
the chunk of plastic, shouting "DIE!"

*Francis Geyer*

# Burning Sappho

The clothes are washed, the house is clean.
I find my pen and start to write.
Something like hatred forks between
my child and me. She kicks her good
new well-selected toys with spite
around the room, and whines for food.
Inside my smile a monster grins
and sticks her image through with pins.

The child is fed, and sleeps. The dishes
are washed, the clothes are ironed and aired.
I take my pen. A kind friend wishes
to gossip while she darns her socks.
Scandal and pregnancies are shared.
The child wakes, and the Rector knocks.
Invisible inside their placid
hostess, a fiend pours prussic acid.

Night now. Orion first begins
to show. Day's trivial angers cease.
All is required, until one wins,
at last, this hour. I start to write.
My husband calls me, rich in peace,
to bed. Now deathless verse, good night.
In my warm thighs a fleshless devil
chops him to bits with hell-cold evil.

All's quiet at last: the world, the flesh,
the devils burning in my brain.
Some air of morning stirs afresh
my shaping element. The mind
with images of love and pain
grapples down gulfs of sleep. I'll find
my truth, my poem, and grasp it yet.
    "The moon is gone, the Pleiads set . . . ."

*Miriam Stone*


# Suburban Sonnet

She practises a fugue, though it can matter
to no one now if she plays well or not.
Beside her on the floor two children chatter,
then scream and fight. She hushes them. A pot
boils over. As she rushes to the stove
too late, a wave of nausea overpowers
subject and counter-subject. Zest and love
drain out with soapy water as she scours
the crusted milk. Her veins ache. Once she played
for Rubinstein, who yawned. The children caper
round a sprung mousetrap where a mouse lies dead.
When the soft corpse won't move they seem afraid.
She comforts them; and wraps it in a paper
featuring: *Tasty dishes from stale bread*.

*Miriam Stone*

# Chance Meeting

I smile. Anger contracts your face.
Two women talking, who might seem
old friends to casual passers-by,
we stand in this familiar place.
Sometimes I meet you in a dream,
here, and all's well. How often I

fashion some god who smiles on me
when smiles are wanting — but such dreams
are faded chromolithotints
reversed from hard reality.
Not love, nor hate, but something streams
between us, as you speak with hints

of knowing this or that which might
hurt me: some brilliance of the mind
that lights us, at whatever cost.
If we were men, perhaps we'd fight,
mop up the blood, let friendship find
more casual ways and not be lost.

You thrash our history for old
misdeeds that hardly bear retracing.
I grin and joke as the words sting.
Really I feel like Archibald
Douglas in heavy armour racing
breathless beside his angry king:

but you're no king, and I'm no knight;
we've no Linlithgow's peace to ride to.
We're women in an elegant war.
The weather goes pathetic; light
turns grey; it's raining. You decide to
drive me. What do you do it for,

knowing too well I know by heart
your bone-clear profile and the way
the hair springs from your brow. We sit
as close as friends, but far apart,
and I'm too close to tears to say
plain words keener than wounding wit:

no one who knows what friendship is
chooses and picks the virtuous;
we love where we must love; so when
we showed ourselves without disguise
friendship itself had chosen us.
I could have hidden from you then

all you reproach me with. You suffer
that knowledge as I suffer still
the self that made my tongue my own
to speak the love I still must offer
whether you wish me well or ill.
You drop me. I walk on alone.

*Miriam Stone*


# Nightfall

*To the memory of Vera Cottew*

Houselights waken. It grows late.
Cold flowers wreathe a ruined gate.
      Over it steps a man.
   Wet sand bursts into flame.

He walks on the deserted shore.
His footsteps mark its burning floor.
    Water walks at his heels
    rustling broken shells.

Layer on layer of gold leaf
peels from the sea. I read his grief
    and its weight which can be told
    from the way his body's held.

This nightfall glow, water's soft lapping
he treads away: a fancy wrapping
    on his world's empty box.
    Declared lifeless by his kicks,

breast upward on the rosy sand,
a parable of old raptures and
    their compensating pain
    a seabird lies. The man

turns, and walks, and turns unseeing.
Light fails. Some density of being
    marks him as he walks on
    when the last light is gone.

In Brisbane twenty years ago
I sat with you, watching the glow
    of calm water at nightfall;
    silent, secure in full

acknowledgment of our unending
heritage; earth's beauty mending
    the miseries of time.
    You suffered. I could not come

a thousand miles, being great with child.
I walked in joy. Your cells ran wild.
    Others held you that day
    when you put brightness by.

Beside your easel once you put
poinsettias and halved fruit,
    and smiling said, "See how
    light speaks always of *now*."

Fruit, flowers. In paint they multiply
the talents of your hand and eye;
    in their still life unite
    vanished and present light.

In deepest solitude we reach
another's. Up and down the beach
    a man walks, bearing in gross
    darkness some mortal loss.

# Four Impromptus

*To Rex Hobcroft*

I

Changed by the fugitive light of dusk
the landscape melts and flows to peace,
but the heart fretting in its husk
of flesh is restless, seeks release.

As a young child I could not bear
to see the sun go down, and I
would pray for endless light; no prayer
could keep the sun firm in the sky

and shadows one by one would claim
my world. At nightfall still, some fear,
some anguish that I cannot name
grips me, and evening finds me here

obscurely troubled, a plain fool
mourning for daylight's transience,
who cannot make of light a tool
to shape joy from the flux of sense.

Wholeness is elsewhere. At this hour
I sense and fear the involving shape
of absence, and a night whose power
the gifts of grace alone escape.

II

Early for my first lesson, afraid to knock,
I waited, an awkward child, outside a room
where scales, while a metronome pulsed like a feverish clock,
unwound their procession of notes; and in the gloom

of that empty hall the sounds turned in my head
to syllables of a language I must make
my own: clear-sounding, as airy and plain as bread
they summoned a hungering child to enter and take

nourishment in a world whose joy transcends
all temporal need, where the heart understands
unquestionable shapes of truth, and mends
its mortal wounds.
                      You enter, and warm your hands

by playing scales, and again as the notes unfold
heart stirs and wakens, waiting to enter in
its passion of sound. I listen, as of old:
this hour will change my life. All's to begin.


III

Those who are lucky find a few:
to the heart's innermost recesses
their words and looks and gestures fall
like light, and this is mutual.

Think of light entering a room:
nothing is asked, and nothing offered;
but mind and eye together wake
to see the commonest objects take

authentic clarity of form,
and fresh from rest the heart embraces
for a brief moment, unafraid,
the stuff of which the world is made.

This day will end. The world will end.
Light changes, and we change and suffer.
But for this hour I offer you,
whose warmth and words and skill renew

the heart, a poem, though words can never
contain, as music does, the unsayable
grace that cannot be defined
yet leaps like light from mind to mind.

IV

Clear, simple as a windless day
calm in its paradise of blue,
when through the quiet of earth it seems
that earth itself will speak to you:

when eyes from every bush and flower
stare into being, and thoughts move
in visions, and love is answered in
the human faces that you love:

clear as a landscape filled with sun
issues this theme, a drift of air
brought into form by mind and hand.
Let heart put off its cloudy care,

rejoice to learn how in the plain
texture of truth its peace is found,
and rest in elemental joy
under this firmament of sound.

# In Brisbane

By the old bridge in flaring sunlight
a ghost is waiting, with my face
of twenty years ago, to show me
the paths I never can retrace.

Here as of old upon the river
float light's beguiling images.
Over a quilt of blue the branches
bend with domestic tenderness.

Here, to my blood's exalted rhythm,
silly with love I'd pace for hours
sifting the piecemeal revelations
of life and time through falling flowers.

Intemperate ghost, who longed to hazard
the pure space of experience,
to bid unheard-of constellations
form from their joyful elements:

these trees that cannot hold their blossom,
the public handsomeness of stone
remain. Your grand abstractions shimmered
like light on water, and are gone.

My ghost, my self, most intimate stranger
standing beneath these lyric trees
with your one wineglassful of morning
snatched from the rushing galaxies,

bright-haired and satin-lipped you offer
the youth I shall not taste again.
I know, I bear to know, your future
unlooked-for love, undreamed-of pain.

With your untempered spirit shatter
the glass of time that keeps apart
what was and is.
                Through fractured sunlight
I see a less-than-shadow pass

to light again. A cloud of blossom
drifts on the water's changing face
from the blue trees unfolding summer
above my head in sunlit space.

# Estuary

*To Rex Hobcroft*

Wind crosshatches shallow water.
Paddocks rest in the sea's arm.
Swamphens race through spiky grass.
A wire fence leans, a crazy stave
with sticks for barlines, wind for song.
Over us, interweaving light
with air and substance, ride the gulls.

Words in our undemanding speech
hover and blend with things observed.
Syllables flow in the tide's pulse.
My earliest memory turns in air:
Eclipse. Cocks crow, as if at sunset;
Grandmother, holding a smoked glass,
says to me, *"Look. Remember this."*

Over the goldbrown sand my children
run in the wind. The sky's immense
with spring's new radiance. Far from here,
lying close to the final darkness,
a great-grandmother lives and suffers,
still praising life: another morning
on earth, cockcrow and changing light.

Over the skeleton of thought
mind builds a skin of human texture.
The eye's part of another eye
that guides it through the maze of light.
A line becomes a firm horizon.
All's as it was in the beginning.
Obscuring symbols melt away.

*"Remember this."* I will remember
this quiet in which the questioning mind
allows reality to enter
its gateway as a friend, unchallenged,
to rest as a friend may, without speaking;
light falling like a benediction
on moments that renew the world.


# Past and Present

I

A fish on my hook thrashed
in its passion of air, and spiked
my finger clean to the bone.
On the phosphorescent browns
and blacks of the rotting pier
my blood fell drop by drop.
You seized my finger and sucked the wound,
and left my hand in yours
as you spoke of the echoes of pigment:
how sunset gashed the west
and my blood cooled on decaying wood
with the selfsame fading colours.
A painter absorbed in light,
and myself, neither woman nor child —
a nest of self-torturing demons —
we sat until darkness fell
and the luminescent water glowed
with thickets of bristling eyes,
and shoreward the seawind breathed
in ribs of inconstant stone.

Between the pulse of the sea
and the quick pulse of my throbbing wound
I felt your life-bright presence drawing
my inward sight to its point of rest.


II  *To Rex Hobcroft*

We walk on this peaceful shore
in the excellence of sunlight.
White hawthorn foams round the houses.
I think of Blake's innocent world
where joy sits on every bough
as your daughter paddles beside us,
amazed at the facts of earth:
at the creatures that glide in her shadow;
at the delicate spines of the dead;
at the surface renewing itself
where she scoops with her hands in the water.
In her wake, like a vision in flux,
a torrent of light streams outward,
and under the fingers of wind
small waves start up in a fugue
of water repeating each shape
in manifold overlapping.

When I walked here last, alone,
it was cold, in the late spring
with Orion back in the sky.
It seemed that one long dead
who had walked with me on another shore
came to my side in darkness.
I walked again with that one
who taught me creation was labour,
who took me beyond the range
of salon pictures and coffee-bar poems

to the passionate patience of art.
I think of the fastness of death.
Of Dietrich Bonhoeffer in prison
remembering a theme:
"Sometimes the music heard
in our inward ear surpasses
the beauty of physical sound.
There is something purer about it."
And perhaps it is so with the dead
when they rise in the mind's image
to walk again with the sharpness of life.

We walk in the present sun
talking of canons and fugues,
art's miracle, which is constant:
that hard-worked artifice
should sound innate, and be music still.
What matter if griefs return
with the spiky thrust of spring?
I know that joy will come
as a voice in a fugue returns
to enter and alter the texture
of accumulating seasons.
I feel time lift and lighten
between the peace of the dead
and the living child beside us
who touches the quick of light.
What's grief but the after-blindness
of the spirit's dazzle of love?

# To Another Poet

I hold in the same thought
a pain now bearable
and what could not be borne.
This evening out of time
we talk: the world is changed
never to be remade
of its old heaviness.

Something that beat in dumb
fury against the glass
of knowing, knows, and is looking
through stillness at this room
where children swarm, whose play
bespeaks our century:
they spread with formal vengeance

armies across the floor.
Across their noise we talk,
drawn to the same enduring
themes with a wakeful joy.
At the fringes of the mind
fragments of thought are stirred
to life, and gather together.

We have no ready-learnt
paraphrase of the world.
Today's love must sustain
today, and no life is made
of manageable stuff.
But this evening I put off
an old tyrannic grief,

and in this usual room,
a place, a field, a world
where children play, I gather
nourishment from another
mind that seeks, and follows
an orbit like my own.
We smile and say goodnight.


# Littoral

*To Rex Hobcroft*

Stones rolled in lively anarchy
through centuries of water grind
these hemispheres in softer stone.
I walk along a narrow ledge
of sandstone at the water's edge,
and thought like water takes its own
shape in the hollows of the mind.
A mile across the river lie

houses and streets, a world away,
where daily I put on the same
mask: my familiar, anti-grand
manner, kindly, responsible —
*dry pebbles in an empty skull
hear the old clichés roll!*
                                 No hand
ravished me from the height I claim.
Freedom is power to choose. Each day

I choose my life, choose to be woven
in other lives, and weave my own

threads in a fabric of such weight
it pulls flesh earthward, yet can lift
a breathing animal to swift
flight from the miseries of fate.
How shall the heart's true shape be known,
spirit made manifest? Beethoven

struggled through temporal misery
to find that form. I think of you
playing those late sonatas fashioned
for a world that will outlast the span
of our own lives, where spirit can
speak of itself, press its impassioned
form upon empty air: each new
theme is a new reality.

Proud of their strength, my children take
turns with the heavy pack, and I
walk light, between the seawind's hum
in airshot cliffs and water's bright
network of overlapping light,
through time where past and future come
to the fine edge of clarity:
a world I never can remake,

a world still to be made. I must
suffer, and change, and question all,
wrestle with thought and word, and bind
my speech to earth's own laws to win
the heart's true life at last.
                                  Once in
a bare room, shaken by the wind
when sunlight shivered and a tall
poplar glittered in shifting dust,

heart leapt beyond music, past the span
of human hands and human skill
to affirm *what is*. My children call
across the wind for me to come;
the tide streams through a honeycomb
of rock and air. This littoral
margin of land and water still
vibrates with life, where life began.

## Alla Siciliana

*To O.B. Dunne*

Earthbound, I watch the darting swallows.
In shivering reeds the wind is caught.
Bright water bears away the mind's
unravellings of restless thought.

Sunset's clear-speaking light discloses
in the calm eloquence of stone,
the lapsing syllables of water,
the whispering reeds and grasses blown

to quiet at last, to windfall silence,
another tongue, a language learned
by ear, by heart in earliest childhood,
when earth in its own radiance turned

always from nightmare-dark to morning.
I see that lost enchantment wake
in light, on water, and the spirit
like a loved guest on earth can take

its needs and its delights, and wander
freely. The dazzling moments burn
to time again. In simple twilight
water speaks peace, the swallows turn

in lessening arcs. The dry reeds rustle
and part to set the nightwind free.
The heart holds, like remembered music,
a landscape grown too dark to see.


# Variations on a Theme

I   Vincent Buckley: *Impromptu on a Nursery Theme*

I might have run with them,
a foreign, panting man,
while round the withered stem
of mulberry they ran.
The weasel first, and then
the gap-toothed monkey went
pulling his green socks up.
Round, round, and round again
with bestial intent.
I gathered in a cup
the improvident fruit that fell
to slake my urgent thirst.
Each in his private hell
they ran. I heard a POP:
Sweet Christ, the weasel burst!

II   Rosemary Dobson: *The Watcher*

In the small garden of my house
  there grows a little mulberry bush
to which two wildwood creatures come.
  In dappled sunlight round they rush.

I often wonder what they seek
  out in the morning's troubled hush,
for I am troubled too, and weak,
  and sometimes beat about the bush.

What is it that the preacher said?
  He said, the race is to the strong.
Brothers, we must by him be led
  to see the monkey's action wrong.

Ah, foolish ape! By worldly care
  too soon oppressed, towards earth he bends.
But poets turn their thoughts to where
  the weasel's life in glory ends.


III   Vivian Smith: *Double Entendre*

They run around the shaking bush.
The mulberries are black with juice.
The anxious desolate monkey stops.
His socks are knitted, torn and loose.

The fragile weasel runs and swells
above the waste of trampled grass,
and tense with unfulfilled despair
explodes in light like broken glass.

IV   James McAuley: *Prefigurations*

On love's elemental course
ran the weasel and the ape,
kept by love's imperious force
in sinuous and in simian shape,
till the monkey found that both
socks were eaten by the moth.

By the ripening mulberry bush
standing silent in the shade,
he wept to hear the weasel push
towards fulfilment, unafraid;
and with one half-naked foot
seized the dark forbidden fruit.

Then the fainting weasel, chased
no longer by mysterious love,
felt the core of life displaced,
fell to earth, and could not move.
Swelled and burst, as in a dream.
Revelation is my theme.


V   A.D. Hope: *A Divination*

True tales and false alike rise to perplex us.
*Putorius nivalis*, chased for hours
by *Simia Satyrus*, runs to vex us
where, under unisexual mulberry flowers,

I stroke your golden loins in virile fashion.
How shall I fable forth my love and grief?
The sad ape stops and stoops to ape my passion.
The weasel pops, in colours past belief.

VI   Francis Geyer: *Bestial Morning*

I remember them, two beasts in your freezing island,
running in endless circles in the sleet.
You with your choir-boy face sat there beside me
knitting warm socks to clothe the monkey's feet.
And the monkey, does he wear the socks you made him?
Does he, like me, from sheer exhaustion stop
to pull them up? And does the weasel follow
his hopeless path or, like my heart, go POP?


VII   Gwen Harwood: *Fuse-Lighting*

Professor Eisenbart, asked to arrest
a monkey and a weasel, turned away.
Under the burning fields of quiet cloud
his mistress munched a mulberry, and pressed
the sour juice on her tongue. The rational day
declined to night's unreason. While the proud

weasel, charged with sinister energy,
ran round the bush, the anonymous monkey, lame
with blistered feet, hitched at one tattered sock.
Eisenbart grinned, and lit a fuse. The tree,
heavy with mulberries, burst into flame.
The weasel felt the great bomb's fatal shock.

# New Music

*To Larry Sitsky*

Who can grasp for the first time
these notes hurled into empty space?
Suddenly a tormenting nerve
affronts the fellowship of cells.
Who can tell for the first time
if it is love or pain he feels,
violence or tenderness that calls
plain objects by outrageous names

and strikes new sound from the old names?
At the service of a human vision,
not symbols, but strange presences
defining a transparent void,
these notes beckon the mind to move
out of the smiling context of
what's known; and what can guide it is
neither wisdom nor power, but love.

Who but a fool would enter these
regions of being with no name?
Secure among their towering junk
the wise and powerful congregate
fitting old shapes to old ideas,
rocked by their classical harmonies
in living sleep. The beggars' stumps
bang on the stones. Nothing will change.

Unless, wakeful with questioning,
some mind beats on necessity,
and being unanswered learns to bear
emptiness like a wound that no
word but its own can mend; and finds
a new imperative to summon
a world out of unmeasured darkness
pierced by a brilliant nerve of sound.

# Poems 1969–1974
from *Selected Poems* (1975)

## Dust to Dust

I dream I stand once more
in Ann Street by the old
fire station. The palms
like feather dusters move
idly in stifling air.
The sky's dusted with gold.
A footfall; someone comes;
I cannot speak for love.

We walk in silence past
All Saints'. The dead do rise,
do live, do walk and wear
their flesh. Your exile's done.
So, so, resume our last
rejoicing kiss. Your eyes
flecked with my image stare
in wonder through my own.

Round us air turns to flame.
Ashes rain from the sky.
A firebell clangs and clangs
insanely as I wake
to absence with your name
shaping my lips. I lie
losing the dream that hangs
fading in air. I shake

the last of night away.
These bright motes that define
morning inside my room
hold not one grain of you.

Another sunstruck day
whose moving dust-motes shine
remote from any dream
cannot restore, renew

our laughter that hot night
when by All Saints' we talked
in the brief time we had.
During *Magnificat*
an urchin stopped to write
on the church wall. He chalked
his message: GOD IS MAD.
I say amen to that.


# An Impromptu for Ann Jennings

Sing, memory, sing those seasons in the freezing
   suburb of Fern Tree, a rock-shaded place
with tree ferns, gullies, snowfalls and eye-pleasing
   prospects from paths along the mountain-face.

Nursing our babies by huge fires of wattle,
   or pushing them in prams when it was fine,
exchanging views on diet, or Aristotle,
   discussing Dr Spock or Wittgenstein,

cleaning up infants and the floors they muddied,
   bandaging, making ends and tempers meet —
sometimes I'd mind your children while you studied,
   or you'd take mine when I felt near defeat;

keeping our balance somehow through the squalling
    disorder, or with anguish running wild
when sickness, a sick joke from some appalling
    orifice of the nightwatch, touched a child;

think of it, woman: each of us gave birth to
    four children, our new lords whose beautiful
tyrannic kingdom might restore the earth to
    that fullness we thought lost beyond recall

when, in the midst of life, we could not name it,
    when spirit cried in darkness, "*I will have . . .*"
but what? have what? There was no word to frame it,
    though spirit beat at flesh as in a grave

from which it could not rise. But we have risen.
    Caesar's we were, and wild, though we seemed tame.
Now we move where we will. Age is no prison
    to hinder those whose joy has found its name.

We are our own. All Caesar's debts are rendered
    in full to Caesar. Time has given again
a hundredfold those lives that we surrendered,
    the love, the fruitfulness; but not the pain.

Before the last great fires we two went climbing
    like gods or blessed spirits in summer light
with the quiet pulse of mountain water chiming
    as if twenty years were one long dreaming night,

above the leafy dazzle of the streams
    to fractured rock, where water had its birth,
and stood in silence, at the roots of dreams,
    content to know: our children walk the earth.

# Matinee

Kröte plays for a tenor bleating
Schubert songs at an Afternoon.
Some idiot biscuit-nibbler beating
time on a saucer with a spoon
makes him accelerate his pace.
Annoyance clouds the tenor's face.

He sings, "My heart is like the sea",
frowning at his accompanist,
but at "where many a pearl may be"
glows, to imply he can't resist
the charm of music-loving girls
who plainly think he's crammed with pearls.

Applause! The singer's head is turned
with praise. Kröte's ignored. "I am
where those young ladies are concerned
only a giant human clam
in whose unlovable inside
dull pearls the size of golf-balls hide."

Hoping by instinct to locate
some drink better than tea, he snatches
the choicest cream-cake from a plate,
and wanders off while no one watches,
licking his fingers, opening doors,
dropping odd crumbs on polished floors

or bedroom carpets. His vain prying
leads him into a nursery
where in its cot a child is crying.
Kröte looks round him guiltily.
Mother? or nurse? No one at all.
How tenderly he lifts the small

creature and soothes it; rearranges
its shawl; so, comforted and kissed,
the fretful baby's crying changes
to trembling smiles. From its plump wrist
dangles a heart-shaped locket set
with pearls. Engraved is: *Margaret*.

"My child. My sister." Kröte sits
beside the window with his prize,
marvelling how her frail skull fits
the hollow of his arm, how wise
yet innocent her glances seem.
He takes her, in his waking dream,

to be his own. Sober, inspired
by his enchanting child, his days
are prodigies of work; admired
by all, he writes, composes, plays
as no one's played before. He sees
his image in the glass, and he's

himself, the man he knows, the same
suburban Orpheus reflected
against a darkening sky, whose name
is called, who knows that he's expected
to play more swan songs. So he lays
his sleeping beauty down, but stays

one moment longer to make sure
her sleep is sound. "So was I, long
ago," he mourns, losing the pure
translucence of her face among
those ignorant of what wonders rest
in his obscure, unfathomed breast.

# Reed Voices

She waits, not far from death,
in her old house by the river.
How the reeds multiply!
They move closer each night
surely, their ghostly plumes
nodding to let the white
heron pass to his nest.
Their delicate armies sway
close-whispering, until the break of day.

What is there to besiege
but an old woman lying
alone, past hope or caring.
with voices in her head
"Not all of us shall die
My love, come to my bed,
and I will give you children.
Let us join in love's play,
lock your limbs close until the break of day."

 "Mother." A child, afraid.
Great with another child
she rises clumsily.
"My dear, I am close by.
Shall we look from the window?"
"There are flowers in the sky."
"We call them stars, night's flowers.
Sleep, sleep, and I will stay
close to your cot until the break of day."

"Mother, it is a daughter.
We shall call her after you."
And that child, bearing children —
her name, her features taken

by wordless naked strangers.
But her life! She feels it shaken
by a strange wind out of time
that stirs the reeds all night.
She hears them whisper until morning light.

Generations of voices
like water-companies streaming
through the shallows of her mind
flash, ripple, and glide on
to healing depths of sleep.
"Children, where have you gone?"
The reeds shake out their plumes.
Their ghost-light armies stay
guarding her sleep until the break of day.


## Winter Quarters

We sit in someone else's house
a-drinking at the dry red wine
after long separation, flaunting
banners of memory with their strange
devices (others watching us
for intimations of some fine
poetic love-death) round the haunting
sense of a time no time can change.

We learn from one involving stare
all men are mortal, and we are
human indeed. The triumphs won
from time remain invisible.

Years that have taught us how to wear
defeat like an old duelling scar
paled to distinction, flash and run
like minutes to this beautiful

half-drunken *now*, where we might be
two captains resting, wearied by
a long campaign, at ease yet still
alert, friends long enough to show
the heart's true gentleness, to see
the mask of day's authority
put by, drinking night's peace until
a word, a look, can say: I know

as I am known. I look. I store
the memory that must serve so long.
Feature by feature I record
your ageing face, through which the loved
unageing spirit shines once more
to liberate the pulse of song
in that calm centre where each word
hangs like a waterdrop unmoved

in early quietness, the real
presence of morning globed in light.
Look long and truthfully. Each scar
declares our living worth. Be sure
that the clean wounds of time will heal.
Rejoice in this unwounded night.
The young are beautiful. We are
ourselves, and love, and will endure.

# The Violets

It is dusk, and cold. I kneel to pick
frail melancholy flowers among
ashes and loam. The melting west
is striped like ice-cream. While I try
whistling a trill, close by his nest
our blackbird frets and strops his beak
indifferent to Scarlatti's song.
Ambiguous light. Ambiguous sky

      Towards nightfall waking from the fearful
      half-sleep of a hot afternoon
      at our first house, in Mitchelton,
      I ran to find my mother, calling
      for breakfast. Laughing, "It will soon
      be night, you goose," her long hair falling
      down to her waist, she dried my tearful
      face as I sobbed, "Where's morning gone?"

and carried me downstairs to see
spring violets in their loamy bed.
Hungry and cross, I would not hold
their sweetness, or be comforted,
even when my father, whistling, came
from work, but used my tears to scold
the thing I could not grasp or name
that, while I slept, had stolen from me

those hours of unreturning light.
Into my father's house we went,
young parents and their restless child,
to light the lamp and the wood stove
while dusk surrendered pink and white
to blurring darkness. Reconciled,

I took my supper and was sent
to innocent sleep.
                    Years cannot move

nor death's disorienting scale
distort those lamplit presences:
        a child with milk and story-book;
        my father, bending to inhale
        the gathered flowers, with tenderness
        stroking my mother's goldbrown hair.
        Stone-curlews call from Kedron Brook.
Faint scent of violets drifts in air.


# Iris

Three years with our three sons you worked to build her,
  named for the rainbow, late and lively child
whom the sea fondles. A fresh breeze has filled her.
  Tension and buoyant ease are reconciled

as she puts off the heavy yoke of land
  and takes the wind's light burden in her sails.
*Ship-shape; an even keel*: we understand
  old clichés truly — sixty pounds of nails

gripping her ribs, six hundredweight of lead
  flourishing water's frail cascading lace.
Age after age the same, still tenanted
  with earth's first creatures, water bears no trace

of time or history on its shining skin.
  Far from the shore where small crabs trim the rotten
scraps from a city's fringes, we begin
  (husband and wife so long we have forgotten

all singularity), our day of rest
   above that element where none sit hand
in hand, salt glitter tossed from crest to crest
   lights nothing of those gulfs where none can stand

upright; here nothing smiles; pity's unknown.
   A crippled gull I found helplessly dying
used its last life to stab me to the bone.
   Some old, lost self strikes from time's shallows, crying

"Beyond habit, household, children, I am I.
   Who knows my original estate, my name?
Give me my atmosphere, or let me die."
   — Give me your hand. The same pure wind, the same

light-cradling sea shall comfort us, who have
   built our ark faithfully. In fugitive
rainbows of spray she lifts, wave after wave,
   her promise: those the waters bear shall live.


## The Flight of the Bumble Bee

Kröte plays for a fiddler scraping
   that Bee Thing from his violin.
There's little prospect of escaping
   back to the Green Room and his gin.

A piece concerned with flight — symbolic!
   he murmurs, pianissimo.
Somebody hisses "Alcoholic"
   audibly from the nearest row.

That woman with the bust! That bumbling
  amateur with an insect heart!
Heaven preserve me from all fumbling
  spear-holders on the stage of Art.

Drunk, often. Alcoholic, never!
  Here come those octaves-and-a-third.
Madam, I could play on for ever,
  thinks Kröte, playing his absurd

pantomime of a great musician
  wrestling hard with his instrument.
The fiddler's nervous disposition
  rapidly throws him off the scent

of any flower the bee might visit —
  he scrapes beyond the normal ear.
Has Kröte drowned him out? Or is it
  a sound that only bats could hear?

The woman with the bust claps brightly,
  not sure that anything's amiss.
The fiddler bows, deciding rightly
  against an encore. Kröte's bliss

flowers in the Green Room, where restored to
  his bottle, in the grateful pause
before the storm, he can afford to
  ignore the honey of applause.

# Night Flight

In the limbo of middle air
  we cruise, drowned in high cloud,
between somewhere and somewhere
  with the old Electra's loud
whine, and the seat-frames creaking,
and "This is your Captain speaking . . ."

Indifferent to night
  the God in the machine
tells us our speed and height,
  names crisply the unseen
landmarks and towns below —
nothing I need to know.

I see those well-known places
  like snatches of old song:
my house, my children's faces;
  late roses left too long
in a rosé bottle, dying.
O, that we two were lying —

O that we two were — Christ,
  what do I want, or need?
Once, when the world sufficed
  I'd sit for hours to read
to a sick child, or spend
evenings, world without end

in children's games, or rest
   like a gentle animal
with a baby at my breast
   watching slow darkness fall,
wrapped in earth's tenderness;
blessed, and with power to bless.


How can this body past
   childbearing lapse and rage,
spirit's fury at last
   quicken, and wreck the cage
of absence, so I stare
across wastes of frozen air? —


barefooted, grave, you stand
   in a room pulsing with wine;
take the glass from my hand,
   and put your hand in mine;
so, like two children playing,
or two court fools displaying


their smiling effigies
   to earnest fools, we dance.
Careless with joy, I seize
   this night's extravagance,
and breathe, as I breathe air,
the world of your despair.


Empty and light, I burn
   with rapture, as of old;
by that heat-lightning learn
   sorrow has taken hold
of this one whom I love.
I feel it, as we move

to *Lucy in the Sky*
   *with Diamonds*, through my skin.
Absorb it, eye to eye;
   suffer it; drink it in;
clasp it, immediate;
fill with it, bear its weight.

Love whom you will. I've known
   enough of love to know
what flesh holds for its own
   in the molten afterglow:
its gulfs of night, immense,
calm, empty, where each sense

surrenders all, as in
   some rapture of the deep;
where soul and body spin
   through the grand depths of sleep:
so I float, for a brief space,
in the dance, in your embrace.

Suffer my love, as I
   suffer myself, still flying
with Lucy in the sky
   among dazzling visions, lying
in half-sleep in mid-air
between nowhere and nowhere.

What's love but this sustaining
   violence — grains of time
igniting, burning, raining
   through absence as I climb
on stormy air to lie
alone in the black sky.

# At Mornington

They told me that when I was taken
to the sea's edge, for the first time,
I leapt from my father's arms
and was caught by a wave and rolled
like a doll among rattling shells;
and I seem to remember my father
fully clothed, still streaming with water
half comforting, half angry.
And indeed I remember believing
as a child, I could walk on water —
the next wave, the next wave —
it was only a matter of balance.

On what flood are they borne,
these memories of early childhood
iridescent, fugitive
as light in a sea-wet shell,
while we stand, two friends of middle age,
by your parents' grave in silence
among avenues of the dead
with their cadences of trees,
marble and granite parting
the quick of autumn grasses.
We have the wholeness of this day
to share as we will between us.

This morning I saw in your garden
fine pumpkins grown on a trellis
so it seemed that the vines were rising
to flourish the fruits of earth
above their humble station
in airy defiance of nature
— a parable of myself,
a skinful of elements climbing

from earth to the fastness of light;
now come to that time of life
when our bones begin to wear us,
to settle our flesh in final shape

as the drying face of land
rose out of earth's seamless waters.
>    I dreamed once, long ago,
>    that we walked among day-bright flowers
>    to a bench in the Brisbane gardens
>    with a pitcher of water between us,
>    and stayed for a whole day
>    talking, and drinking the water.
>    Then, as night fell, you said
>    > "There is still some water left over."

We have one day, only one,
but more than enough to refresh us.

At your side among the graves
I think of death no more
than when, secure in my father's arms,
I laughed at a hollowed pumpkin
with candle flame for eyesight,
and when I am seized at last
and rolled in one grinding race
of dreams, pain, memories, love and grief,
from which no hand will save me,
the peace of this day will shine
like light on the face of the waters
that bear me away for ever.

# David's Harp

Saturday morning. I rehearse
the Sunday hymns, fortissimo,
in the cool twilight of the church,
adding new stops at every verse.
Someone creaks the west door. I know
I am the object of his search,
gazed at, as though from far away.
He must be thirty, if a day.

I turn my seventeen-year-old
profile a trifle heavenwards,
and hastily reduce the sound,
accommodating to his bold
descant on *David's Harp*. The Lord's
house might as well be Circe's ground.
"With thee all night I mean to stay,
and wrestle till the break of day."

"With thee all night." So Wesley wrote,
though not with secular intent.
What flourishes that tune will bear!
My tenor wreathes it note by note
in rich Handelian ornament.
Faint burnt-out incense on the air
offends his Presbyterian nose.
He sneezes, stares across the rows

of empty pews between us; still
singing, walks to the organ; stands
beside me; puts his arms around
my waist and squeezes me until

I gasp, then gently lifts my hands
to his, and kisses me. He's sound
of wind. His kiss is long. We share
at last a common need for air.

"Give me one kiss, my bonny lass!"
Vain as a cat, I frown and toss
my head. He watches Brisbane's hot
sunshine, strained through Victorian glass,
lacquer a Station of the Cross.
He scowls and thunders: "Thou shalt not
make any graven images."
But as he bends his head to kiss

the image of his hope, the door
moves with its useful warning creak.
He steps aside. I start to play.
He fills his lungs, and sings once more,
"Speak to me now, in blessings speak."
A death-pale curate come to pray
kneels, and is forced to find his Lord
through a loud F sharp major chord.

Where's that bright man who loved me, when
there was not much to love? He died
soon after. The undying flow
of music bears him close again,
handsome and young, while I am tried
in time's harsh fires. Dear man, I know
your worth, being now less ignorant of
the nature and the names of love.

# Carnal Knowledge I

Roll back, you fabulous animal
be human, sleep. I'll call you up
from water's dazzle, wheat-blond hills,
clear light and open-hearted roses,
this day's extravagance of blue
stored like a pulsebeat in the skull.

Content to be your love, your fool,
your creature tender and obscene
I'll bite sleep's innocence away
and wake the flesh my fingers cup
to build a world from what's to hand,
new energies of light and space

wings for blue distance, fins to sweep
the obscure caverns of your heart,
a tongue to lift your sweetness close
leaf-speech against the window-glass
a memory of chaos weeping
mute forces hammering for shape

sea-strip and sky-strip held apart
for earth to form its hills and roses
its landscape from our blind caresses,
blue air, horizon, water-flow,
bone to my bone I grasp the world.
But what you are I do not know.

# Carnal Knowledge II

Grasshoppers click and whirr.
Stones grow in the field.
Autumnal warmth is sealed
in a gold skin of light
on darkness plunging down
to earth's black molten core.

Earth has no more to yield.
Her blond grasses are dry.
    Nestling my cheek against
    the hollow of your thigh
    I lay cockeyed with love
    in the most literal sense.

Your eyes, kingfisher blue.
This was the season, this
the light, the halcyon air.
Our window framed this place.
If there were music here,
insectile, abstract, bare,

it would bless no human ear.
Shadows lie with the stones.
Bury our hearts, perhaps
they'll strike it rich in earth's
black marrow, crack, take root,
bring forth vines, blossom, fruit.

    Roses knocked on the glass.
    Wine like a running stream
    no evil spell could cross
    flowed round the house of touch.
God grant me drunkenness
if this is sober knowledge,

song to melt sea and sky
apart, and lift these hills
from the shadow of what was,
and roll them back, and lie
in naked ignorance
in the hollow of your thigh.

# Night Thoughts: Baby & Demon

Baby I'm sick. I need
nursing. Give me your breast.
My orifices bleed.
I cannot sleep. My chest
shakes like a window. Light
guts me. My head's not right.

Demon, we're old, old chap.
Born under the same sign
after some classic rape.
Gemini. Yours is mine.
Sickness and health. We'll share
the end of this affair.

Baby, I'm sick to death.
But I can't die. You do
the songs, you've got the breath.
Give them the old soft shoe.
Put on a lovely show.
Put on your wig, and go.

The service station flags, denticulate
plastic, snap in the wind. Hunched seabirds wait

for light to quench the unmeaning lights of town.
This day will bring the fabulous summer down.

Weather no memory can match will fade
to memory, leaf-drift in the pines' thick shade.

All night salt water stroked and shaped the sand.
All night I heard it. Your bravura hand

chimed me to shores beyond time's rocking swell.
The last cars leave the shabby beach motel.

Lovers and drunks unroofed in sobering air
disperse, ghost-coloured in the streetlight-glare.

> Rock-a-bye Baby
>   in the motel
> Baby will kiss
>   and Demon will tell.

One candle lights us. Night's cool airs begin
to lick the luminous edges of our skin.

> When the bough bends
>   the apple will fall
> Baby knows nothing
>   Demon knows all.

Draw up the voluptuously crumpled sheet.
In rose-dark silence gentle tongues repeat
the body's triumph through its grand eclipse.
I feel your pulsebeat through my fingertips.

>    Baby's a rocker
>       lost on the shore.
>    Demon's a mocker.
>       Baby's a whore.

World of the happy, innocent and whole:
the body's the best picture of the soul
couched like an animal in savage grace.
Ghost after ghost obscures your sleeping face.

>   My baby's like a bird of day
>      that flutters from my side,
>   my baby's like an empty beach
>      that's ravished by the tide.

>   So fair are you, my bonny lass,
>      so sick and strange am I,
>   that I must lie with all your loves
>      and suck your sweetness dry.

>   And drink your juices dry, my dear,
>      and grind your bones to sand,
>   then I will walk the empty shore
>      and sift you through my hand.

And sift you through my hand, my dear,
  and find you grain by grain,
and build your body bone by bone
  and flesh those bones again,

with flesh from all your loves, my love,
  while tides and seasons stream,
until you wake by candle-light
  from your midsummer dream,

and like some gentle creature meet
  the huntsman's murderous eye,
and know you never shall escape
  however fast you fly.

Unhoused I'll shout my drunken songs
  and through the streets I'll go
compelling all I meet to toast
  the bride they do not know.

Till all your tears are dry, my love,
  and your ghosts fade in the sun.
Be sure I'll have your heart, my love,
  when all your loving's done.


# Meditation on Wyatt I

*Whoso list to hunt*

Here and everywhere I meet your crazy scent
except in dreams — you are too near to dream —
I split envelopes and you fall out

introducing your music, such operatic flowers
in the fields of discourse! Your dashes and stops!
Whose is the emblem of a running hound?

I have your world either side of my nose,
to heel! to heel!     my sealcoat shining
through harping grasses     the fields breathe open

I root and feast     no respecter of persons
the rankbrained rulers     rankriding bitches
swallowed     the festering single eye

down and out           deep and bitter the taste
I have run through your dream and muzzle you out
to groundlevel light and lie on your belly

silky and patient         and the dim people
sketch us in pencil, Master and Faithful Hound.
When the horn blows we are equal to that sound.


## Meditation on Wyatt II

"Forget not yet, forget not this"
        We are what darkness has become:
        two bodies bathed in saffron light
        disarmed by sudden distances
        pitched on the singing heights of time
        our skin aflame with eastern airs,
        changed beyond reason, but not rhyme.

"The which so long hath thee so loved"
        counting the pulsebeats        foot to foot
        our splendid metres        limb to limb
        sweet assonance of tongue and tongue
        figures of speech to speech        bemused
        with metaphors as unimproved
        as the crooked roads of genius

        but our hearts' rhymes are absolute.

# Fido's Paw Is Bleeding

Fido's paw is bleeding.
Fido's master finds the cut,
puts a nice clean bandage on,
gives his pet a slice of meat.

Fido's paw is hurting.
Fido cannot offer proof.
Fido's master tries to ease it
when his dog begins to whimper
how could he withhold belief?

Master's heart is broken.
Master's mistress left his roof.
Did she find his house oppressive?
Who can tell — she would not speak,
simply packed her gear and left.
Polly screeches, "Shut your beak!"
Polly isn't talking sense.

Fido's paw is better,
but he whimpers round the house.
Who could teach him this pretence?
Polly goes on screeching.
Master writes a lyric poem
so his pain is manifest.
Polly scatters seed and swears.
Master's mistress taught the bird
language hardly fit for use.

Fido in his kennel
makes no claims about the world.
Master gets a blanket,
throws it over Polly's cage.
Out of doors the rising moon

flames above earth's darkening rim
lifts a yellow eye aloft.
Master in his lonely room
counts the wingbeats of his pain
pours another glass of wine
on the dryness of his song.
Wonders where it all went wrong.


## "Thought Is Surrounded by a Halo"

—Ludwig Wittgenstein, *Philosophical Investigations 97*

Show me the order of the world,
the hard-edge light of this-is-so
prior to all experience
and common to both world and thought,
no model, but the truth itself.

> Language is not a perfect game,
> and if it were, how could we play?
> The world's more than the sum of things
> like moon, sky, centre, body, bed,
> as all the singing masters know.

> Picture two lovers side by side
> who sleep and dream and wake to hold
> the real and the imagined world
> body by body, word by word
> in the wild halo of their thought.

# Father and Child

I   *Barn Owl*

Daybreak: the household slept.
I rose, blessed by the sun.
A horny fiend, I crept
out with my father's gun.
Let him dream of a child
obedient, angel-mild —

old No-Sayer, robbed of power
by sleep. I knew my prize
who swooped home at this hour
with daylight-riddled eyes
to his place on a high beam
in our old stables, to dream

light's useless time away.
I stood, holding my breath,
in urine-scented hay,
master of life and death,
a wisp-haired judge whose law
would punish beak and claw.

My first shot struck. He swayed,
ruined, beating his only
wing, as I watched, afraid
by the fallen gun, a lonely
child who believed death clean
and final, not this obscene

bundle of stuff that dropped,
and dribbled through loose straw
tangling in bowels, and hopped
blindly closer. I saw

those eyes that did not see
mirror my cruelty

while the wrecked thing that could
not bear the light nor hide
hobbled in its own blood.
My father reached my side,
gave me the fallen gun.
"End what you have begun."

I fired. The blank eyes shone
once into mine, and slept.
I leaned my head upon
my father's arm, and wept,
owl-blind in early sun
for what I had begun.


II  *Nightfall*

Forty years, lived or dreamed:
what memories pack them home.
Now the season that seemed
incredible is come.
Father and child, we stand
in time's long-promised land.

Since there's no more to taste
ripeness is plainly all.
Father, we pick our last
fruits of the temporal.
Eighty years old, you take
this late walk for my sake.

Who can be what you were?
Link your dry hand in mine,
my stick-thin comforter.
Far distant suburbs shine
with great simplicities.
Birds crowd in flowering trees,

sunset exalts its known
symbols of transience.
Your passionate face is grown
to ancient innocence.
Let us walk for this hour
as if death had no power

or were no more than sleep.
Things truly named can never
vanish from earth. You keep
a child's delight for ever
in birds, flowers, shivery-grass —
I name them as we pass.

*"Be your tears wet?"* You speak
as if air touched a string
near breaking-point. Your cheek
brushes on mine. Old king,
your marvellous journey's done.
Your night and day are one

as you find with your white stick
the path on which you turn
home with the child once quick
to mischief, grown to learn
what sorrows, in the end,
no words, no tears can mend.

from *The Lion's Bride* (1981)

# The Lion's Bride

I loved her softness, her warm human smell,
her dark mane flowing loose. Sometimes stirred by
rank longing laid my muzzle on her thigh.
Her father, faithful keeper, fed me well,
but she came daily with our special bowl
barefoot into my cage, and set it down:
our love feast. We became the talk of town,
brute king and tender woman, soul to soul.

Until today: an icy spectre sheathed
in silk minced to my side on pointed feet.
I ripped the scented veil from its unreal
head and engorged the painted lips that breathed
our secret names. A ghost has bones, and meat!
Come soon my love, my bride, and share this meal.


# Dialogue

If an angel came with one wish
I might say, deliver that child
who died before birth, into life.
Let me see what she might have become.
He would bring her into a room
fair skinned      the bones of her hands
would press on my shoulderblades
in our long embrace

                        we would sit
with the albums spread on our knees:
now here are your brothers      and here
your sister here the old house

among trees and espaliered almonds.
  — But where am I?
                        Ah my dear
I have only one picture
                 here
in my head     I saw you lying
still folded    one moment    forever
your head bent down to your heart
eyes closed on unspeakable wisdom
your delicate frog-pale fingers

                              spread

apart as if you were playing
a woodwind instrument.

   — My name?
                      It was never given.
  — Where is my grave?


                in my head     I suppose
the hospital burnt you.
  — Was I beautiful?
                  To me.
  — Do you mourn for me every day?
Not at all     it is more than thirty years
I am feeling the coolness of age
the perspectives of memory change.
Pearlskull     what lifts you here
from night-drift to solemn ripeness?
Mushroom dome? Gourd plumpness?
The frog in my pot of basil?

  — It is none of these, but a rhythm
    the bones of my fingers      dactylic
    rhetoric smashed from your memory.
    Forget me again.

     Had I lived
 no rhythm would be the same
 nor my brothers and sister feast
 in the world's eternal house.

Overhead   wings of cloud
    burning   and under my feet
     stones marked with demons' teeth.


# The Silver Swan

"Dietrich!" Someone says Kröte's name.
He is standing in a small museum
by a nineteenth century piano.
Before his time, yet made for him:
how could the vanished craftsman know?
Beyond the usual height, the frame

extends to house a charming cupboard
with curtains of green silk, in which
brandy and glasses are displayed.
— A cabinet-maker born, not made,
like a child blessed with perfect pitch,
he muses. Can't believe he heard

his name, but turns to see beside him
a dowdy woman with a small
schoolboy. Who is it? Names elude him
so often now. "I shouldn't call
you Dietrich, I should say Professor."
She smiles, and he remembers her.

How could that brilliant girl become
this shabby housewife? "The first time
I saw this instrument I thought
of you," she says. "I love this room.
It's years now since I've played a note.
Children, and housework — well, it's grim.

Sometimes I come in here to dream
in silence — an automaton
standing still in a music room.
How strange that we should meet again!
How I loved you when I was young.
I'd often get my fingering wrong

just to get you to hold my hand.
I had a schoolgirl crush on you."
The child fidgets and sniffs. They move
out to the entrance hall, then stand
silent. Those eyes, astonished blue,
now find him *old*. — Who could believe

this was the gifted child who stood
in hospital beside his bed
consumed with total love; who would
learn a sonata in three days —
"I practised till my fingers bled."
Inside its black and silver case

the Swan, a famed automaton,
waits mutely for its next performance.
"Perhaps it was a real swan once,"
the child says. "Well, it carries on,"
the woman sighs, "it moves its wings
and neck and head. But never sings."

Kröte says, "Tell the little chap
that swans sing only when they're dying."
The infant plainly thinks he's lying,
and says so, rudely. Kröte's scowl
rebukes him, a resounding slap
from Mother brings a startling howl.

"We'll have to go." She says goodbye
and promises to keep in touch,
without intent. Dear Dietrich . . . Never.
That time is gone from time forever.
— Is loneliness a gift that I
was born with, like my perfect pitch?

The Swan bends down its head and catches
a fish, while moving rods of glass
ripple like water in a frame
of silver leaves. As Kröte watches,
something cries from the past, Alas!
in the light voice that called his name.

# A Scattering of Ashes

Music alone can make me hold
my breath, thinks Kröte as he catches
his bus. A chill wind sighs. Bone cold
he rubs his hands as something scratches
a blank part of his memory.
Today's not right. Where should he be?

>   Beethoven's funeral. Torchbearer
>   Schubert held lilies bound in black;
>   afterwards with Randhartinger

and Lachner, heavy of heart, went back
to the Mehlgruber Inn, to toast
the one whom death would summon first.

Schubert himself.
                        Kröte recalls
why death is showing him its sting,
and why he thinks of funerals:
he must attend a Scattering
of Ashes, is engaged to play
at the crematorium today.

There he arrives immersed in gloom.
An earlier customer's not through.
The mourners, in a waiting room,
wait, since there's nothing else to do.
An old lady leans close to say,
"My beloved friend knew Massenet."

Kröte's impressed. "And Saint-Saëns too.
She was in Fauré's singing class.
Now I don't know what I shall do.
I thought I'd be the first to pass
away. We were friends for fifty years."
She weeps, and Kröte's close to tears.

They are summoned. Kröte lifts the lid
of a fancy electronic job.
Is this an organ? God forbid.
He fiddles off a plastic knob,
fumbles the pedals with cold feet,
plays what's required, and takes a seat

beside Old Friend while prayers are said.
The chapel's neutral, shiny-clean.
No reason here to bow the head.
What God would visit this cool scene?
— O for a gorgeous requiem.
Old mittened claws: he watches them

extract from her capacious purse
a small carved wooden box, maybe
a reliquary made to nurse
an ash or two? She taps his knee
and puts the casket, like a grand
actress, in his unwilling hand.

— Pins? Needles? "Whiskers! Our dead cats.
We've made provision in our wills
for those outliving us." She pats
his hand confidingly. He spills
the box and contents on the floor.
Mourners are filing through a door,

but Kröte's kneeling to retrieve
whiskers. The cat is on the mat.
Lord, help me find them. I'll believe
in the resurrection of the cat.
She whispers on without concern,
"We couldn't keep whole cats to burn.

Yes, fifty years we lived together.
Cats were our children." Kröte leads
her gently into funeral weather
just as an unseen agent feeds
the ashes from a cross-shaped vent.
She shakes her casket. Whiskers sent

flying off on a sudden gust
fall on the unsuspecting crowd.
— Whiskers to whiskers, dust to dust.
"The Cat's Fugue!" she exclaims aloud.
Kröte begins to hum the theme
and feels her crazy joke redeem

the dismal day. He takes her arm.
She smiles at him, and he can guess
how bright she was, how full of charm.
— Such intervals! Let music bless
all hopes, all loves, however odd.
Music, my joy, my full-scale God.


# A Music Lesson

Kröte's not well. His mood is bloody.
A pupil he can hardly stand
attacks a transcendental study.
— Lord, send me one real pianist.
Soul of a horse! He shapes her hand
and breathes apologies to Liszt.

"Reflect: in order to create
we must know how to. Think about
the balance between height and weight,
shoulder to fingertip; a hanging
bridge, resilient, reaching out
with firm supports. Let's have no banging!

Playing begins inside your brain.
Music's much more than flesh and bone.

Relax, and listen. If you strain
your muscles *here* and *here* contract.
You get a stiff, unlovely tone."
His pupil says, "Is that a fact?"

She plays the passage louder, faster;
indeed deliberately tries
to infuriate her music master.
"The year that Liszt was born, a comet
blazed over European skies."
"Am I to draw conclusions from it?

And, if so, what?" the tyro sneers.
— Cold heart, stiff hands. How to explain?
"When a new genius appears
it's like that fiery head of light
drawing us in its golden train.
Now, shall we try to get it right?

Does it give you no pride to say
'My teacher's teacher learned from Liszt?'
Feel in your hands, before you play,
the body's marvellous architecture:
the muscles between hand and wrist
kept flexible; now try to picture

the finger forming, from the point
where it rests on the key, an arc
curving through every finger-joint,
supporting the whole arm's free weight.
Now the least effort makes its mark.
The instrument can sing."
                             "I'm late,"

the pupil whines. The lesson's over.
The teacher pours himself a gin,

pats the piano like a lover
(— Dear mistress, we're alone once more).
Liszt, with his upper lip gone in,
beams from the cover of a score.

Abbé, forsooth! A toast to you,
old friend, old fiend in monkish dress.
I know you had your off days too.
At Schumann's, Clara said, you played
his work so badly once (confess!)
that only her good manners made

her sit in silence in that room.
— Have mercy on all pianists,
Architect of the world, of whom
I ask that I may live to see
Halley's Comet.
>*If God exists
then music is his love for me.*


# Oyster Cove Pastorals

I *To the Muse*

My fowls with heroes' names,
Hector, Achilles, Ajax,
crow me out to the pasture.
Helios gilds their plumes.
Fossickers in the rye,
they trust me with the axe.

If by some chance I wrote
a fine immortal poem
it would have a mortal theme.
All that excess of life
in museums of the mind
still there to contemplate!

Light fits a world together
from fragments of a dream:
another place, another
morning; a motto: *Summa
Supremo*, best and ablest.
Some happiness is forecast.

What consent do we ever
give to dreams that embrace us
with the energy of art?
Why do you come at morning
when frosty air is burning
my empty arms? I split

wood, light the day's fire,
warm my body at flame
invisible in sunlight.
That brief motto in Latin,
on what door was it written?
Tell me, what is your name?


II  *High Noon*

Ocean, heaven, the same colour.
Bruny lies between
unruffled sky, unclouded water.
Colours of solitude surround us.

Shadows of gentle green
brush the planes of thigh and shoulder.

In this room a whispered name will answer
the soft-spoken address
of eye and lip and loving gesture.
No need for language, the great mirror,
when the body's genius
lights us past logic into rapture.

<u>Instrument and interpreter,</u>
we are one: talk idly, improvise.
    "How will you paint me this green air
    and the distant fields' autumnal shimmer?"
    — As you will sing a dream of leaves
    through which the heavens fall like water.


III   *Evening:"Et in Arcadia ego"*

Even here, in Arcady, are graves:
the mortal part of Gabriel Fur;
Big White the leghorn; old Artemis,
smallest of bantam hens, and her
arch-enemy the feral cat;
the odd wren, the bright pardalote
and the fantail with his cinnamon breast
who stooped to fly clean through the house
and struck the mystery of glass;
gone to their everlasting rest.

Look, where the grass grows more intense:
a bluetongue's skeleton recounts
his lost encounter with the fence.
If there were reason to give thanks
I'd say, earth gathers in her children

and all are equal, born again.
New dreams fire upwards in her thought —
That's earth's religion: fowl to iris,
cat to fresh catmint, lizard to grass,
grass back to geese in a fresh start.

Insect-spires, grass-heads, complex clouds:
nothing but light and surfaces
as the day dies. Autumnal shades
make substance possible. Come close,
friends, lovers, nightfall-visitors
from earlier times. My body wears
the light and substance of the dead.
Daughters and sons of Artemis
come close, and you, my hungry geese.
Here's wheat. The living must be fed.

## Wittgenstein and Engelmann

Olmutz, Moravia: Wittgenstein
  is walking side by side
with Engelmann, who lived to write
  after his friend had died,

"I sought, between the world that is
  and the world that ought to be,
in my own troubled self the source
  of the discrepancy,

and in his lonely mind this touched
  a sympathetic chord.
I offered friendship, and was given
  his friendship, a reward

no gift of mine could match." They walk
  as friends do, late at night,
two men of cultivated taste
  talking, in reason's light,

of music (Wittgenstein had learned
  to play the clarinet;
could whistle, too, in perfect pitch,
  one part from a quartet)

and of the pure veracity
  Wittgenstein prized in art.
'Count Eberhard's Hawthorn', Uhland's poem,
  profoundly touched his heart:

Felicitous, simple: Eberhard
  rode by a hawthorn spray,
and in his iron helmet placed
  a tender sprig of may,

which, preserved through the wars, he brought
  home from his pilgrimage.
It grew into a branching tree
  to shelter his old age.

Above his dreams a flowering arch
  by whispering breezes fanned
recalled the far time when he was
  young, in the Holy Land.

One day when Wittgenstein was ill
  and could not leave his bed,
Engelmann's mother sent her son
  with gruel to see him fed.

Engelmann climbing up the stairs
  slipped with the saucepan full,
and steaming oatmeal porridge splashed
  his coat of threadbare wool.

"You are showering me with kindnesses,"
  said grateful Wittgenstein,
and Engelmann, "I am showering,
  it seems, this coat of mine."

— *He was mightily amused*. The stiff
  unfunny joke survives
through solemn reminiscences
  to illuminate two lives.

Philosopher and architect
  walk through the flaking town,
Wittgenstein in his uniform
  of red and chocolate brown,

formal and courteous they talk
  of the Count's hawthorn flower;
how nature and our thought conform
  through words' mysterious power;

how propositions cannot state
  what they make manifest;
of the ethical and mystical
  that cannot be expressed;

how the world is on one side of us,
  and on the other hand
language, the mirror of the world;
  and God is, *how things stand.*

Europe lies sick in its foul war.
  Armies choke in clay.
But these friends keep their discourse clear
  as the white hawthorn spray,

one a great genius, and both
  humble enough to seek
the simple sources of that truth
  whereof one cannot speak.


# A Valediction

As always after partings, I
get from its place the Oxford Donne,
inked in with aches from adolescence.

Who needs drugs if she has enough
uppers and downers in her head?
Though names are not engraved herein,

who can be literally dead
if he leaps from an underlining
into my flesh at *The Sunne Rising*?

Lou Salomé in her old age: "Whether
I kissed Nietzsche on Monte Sacro
I find I do not now remember."

Young Saint Thérèse of Lisieux, writing
"When I love, it is forever."
One mistress of half Europe, one

enclosed with a transcendent lover.
Dear ladies, shall we meet halfway
between sanctity and liberation?

Today I leave the book unopened.
Strangely, this farewell's left me joyful.
Can ghosts die? Yes, old ghosts are summoned

back to their shades of ink. My lover
will come again to me, my body
to its true end will give him joy.

Now in his absence let me walk
at peaceful sunset in the pasture
feeding my geese, my latter children,

and when the afterglow is gone
Lou's ravishing forgetfulness
will rock my soul with saving laughter,

and the singlehearted saint will braid
all loves into one everlasting.
Then, if I need a lullaby,

good Doctor Donne, will you attend?


# A Morning Air

Two gulls wheel in autumnal air
like souls possessed on this cold shore
crying, crying as if we could
deliver them from Tartarus.

A crust brings them to quiet. Your lips
touch mine with pain and tenderness.
Hunger and solitude are gone.
This moment is the end of time.

There is a death that we live through,
a death we can experience.
Possessing and surrendering
spirit outstrips all understanding.

As light opens to other light
dry grasses sigh like heavy wheat.
We are roofed with silver. Wingbeats rise
from the sea's pure and ardent pulse.


# A Little Night Music

Listen, I will remind you
of what you have never known.
That's what our dreams are for,
and I will be your dream,
a ravishing latecomer
under your handsome skin.
Late, late this night I'll find you

where nothing has a name,
where any page you turn
will long have lost its meaning.
Remember me, while music
melts you to understanding.
Sleep, while new planets burn,
and I will be your dream.

Frost ghosts autumnal pastures.
Though my step is light, my geese
sound their alarm, the plover
scream at me, an intruder
in sleepless fields, and over
your absence measureless
silence extends the stars.



## The Sea Anemones

Grey mountains, sea and sky. Even the misty
seawind is grey. I walk on lichened rock
in a kind of late assessment, call it peace.
Then the anemones, scarlet, gouts of blood.
There is a word I need, and earth was speaking.
I cannot hear. These seaflowers are too bright.
Kneeling on rock, I touch them through cold water.
My fingers meet some hungering gentleness.
A newborn child's lips moved so at my breast.
I woke, once, with my palm across your mouth.
> The word is: *ever*. Why add salt to salt?
> Blood drop by drop among the rocks they shine.
> *Anemos*, wind. The spirit, where it will.

Not flowers, no, animals that must eat or die.

# Death Has No Features of His Own

Death has no features of his own.
He'll take a young eye bathed in brightness
and the raging cheekbones of a raddled queen.
Misery's cured by his appalling taste.
His house is without issue. He appears
garlanded with lovebirds, hearts and flowers.
Anything, everything.
                                      He'll wear my face and yours.
Not as we were, thank God. As we shall be
when we let go of the world, late ripe fruit falling.
What we are is beyond him utterly.


# Beyond Metaphor

Sometimes I'm gripped by poems so sad and awful
I could not write them down. They're like those dreams
you have of irremediable anguish
but can't recount, though you were there, you suffered
your lost love's pain, your child's unanswered cry.
Only Mozart, perhaps, found the right tone
to make things bearable. Who was it said
of the end of the *Tractatus*: What you can't say
you can't say, and you can't whistle it either.

# Andante

New houses grasp our hillside,
my favourite walks are fenced.
Still there's the foreshore, still
transparent overlappings
seaward, let there be space
for the demon's timeless patience
with myself and my dying.

Silence fixes our loves.
Let me cultivate silence.
What's my head but a rat's nest
of dubious texts? Let water
ask me, what have you learned?
I tell the plush deeps, nothing.
Nightfall, an old vexed hour.

Why do I have an image
of owls with silver bells
hung from the tarsus, hunting
fieldmice round the new houses?
Hunger, music and death.
And after that the calm
full frontal stare of silence.

# Seven Philosophical Poems

*To Edwin Tanner*


I  *Ephemeron*

Man, there's a fly in that
bottle. He can't buzz off.
His name's the verb he needs.
He's oblivious to advice,
and if he should drift free
he still will have learned nothing.
But then, he's just a fly.
Up-end it, tip him out.
Let him rejoice and die.


II  *Being in the World*

Alone behind the wheel
half-stupid with fatigue
I fell briefly asleep
on the Midland Highway. God
or someone slapped my life
back in my empty hands
before metal shaped my ends.
Now there's iron in my soul.
Iron in my tongue, too,
clapping against the skull.
Somebody, something loves me
enough to keep me here.
Let my enemies take care.

III  *Burning the Radiata*

Burning the young straight trees I think of you
painting. I know your pain is exquisite.
Not angst, but anguish, pure and physical.
Shoulder, arm, hand: pain flows through to your brush-tip
and there is changed. Colours unlatched from space
alight on canvas, sing the light of reason,
sing vision stripped and still for eye's true mind.
   Find other homes, you birds. In any bushfire
these pines would take us with them. As they fall
air lapses through them like a dying breath.
Their green burns white, then red-gold. They expire
with incense, and a sound of rushing wind.


IV  *Religious Instruction*

My friend and I, put out
from the Old Testament
lesson for giggling, went
and made ourselves from clay
a fine hermaphrodite
idol: huge breasts, the lot.

We sought protection from
teachers and clergymen,
but most, two goatish boys
who took the same road home
calling, "You've got a womb!
Girls have got wombs!" and worse.

Immediate success!
That self-same day the first
caught smoking was well thrashed,
and the second savaged by
a dog he used to tease.
Versions of this got round.

So we reigned in a blessed
communion of young sinners,
queens of the underworld.
But in secret crumbled God
back to his elements
among riddles never guessed.

V   *A Dream*
*Has the verb "to dream" a present tense?*
—Wittgenstein

I see my lover in a field of women
and William Morris flowers. The women are
rose-white and elegant. I run to meet him.
He steps back, saying "Things are not the same."
I say, "You loved me once." He replies coldly,
"I made you love me, knowing I would need
a graft to both big toes. I knew you'd give me
the softest, whitest parts of your own skin."
I am furious, and raise a hand to strike him.
He leans closer and sighs, "My feet are hurting."
I am cold with rage. I shout, "Sir Rat is whining!"
The women drop his arms, and glow with laughter.
Then he comes close, and strokes me, as of old.
His lips against my ear, he breathes, "I made you
love me so that I could write about it."
This seems so reasonable that I smile.
All is forgiven. But all is not the same.

VI  *A Dream of Wittgenstein*

I am in Vienna, in a cobbled street.
It is evening. On a wall a notice says
"Tonight the anthem will be whistled by
Ludwig Wittgenstein." I am dream-weightless
and float to the church door. I find it locked,
but hear his whistling, Mahler-ish, immensely
lonely and grand. A grave procession comes
out of the church. They pass me without seeing:
Engelmann, Schnitzler, Loos, his three doomed brothers,
last, Wittgenstein himself. My wish is granted
if only in a dream. Before he turns
the corner that will take him from my sight
he looks at me. His look says, *You are known*.


VII  *Some Thoughts in the 727*

Wittgenstein once said he wrote
for men who'd breathe a different air.
Did his truth-tables tell him this,
or his beloved composer, Schubert?
Or did the birds of Galway bear
a note to his pure seriousness?

On metal wings a mortal frost
high above summer. Landscape shown
like a child's picture book. I hear
those names whose power can not be lost
bridging the known and the unknown
and feel the sense of life is clear.

# The Wasps

*To Edwin Tanner*

Take up your brush, beloved artist,
  paint me a devil forced to wear
a dress of lavender crochet, picture
  the broomstick limbs and flaming hair.

It is Sunday: a child's Sunday pictures
  lie scattered in loose-fingered grass.
Lolly-coloured assorted faces
  beam at what God has brought to pass.

Under an orange tree her brother
  waddles and crows, absurdly fat.
No godhead skims those rosy features.
  Who said, *Be thou on earth* to that?

Bright from horizon to horizon
  God's eyespace brims with Sunday prayer.
Somewhere above the blue sits Jesus,
  light streaming from his ginger hair.

You told me once you saw in childhood
  a vitreous floater in the sky,
believed it Jesus, and determined
  he should not enter through your eye.

Your brother (Cain? or Abel?) and a
  goanna in the orchard were
enough of scripture when you hunted
  the sky in vain for Lucifer.

Two children of the Devil's party —
  the years frog-march us place by place
to meet in middle life, still probing
  the ambiguities of space.


The sorcerer's apprentice, loathing
  her rival in his harmless play,
implores the Friend of Little Children
  to take and keep him far away.


His plump hand rests in hers. She leads him
  across forbidden garden beds
to trample on the Jesus-gentle
  flowers, and strew their torn-off heads


along the orchard path. No murmur
  comes from the Sinner's Friend on high.
They reach the shadowy barn and stand there
  roofed from the wrath of God's blue eye.


High on a cross-beam, wasps, entombing
  a lightless banquet for their young,
flourish their tiger-stripes to menace
  a child armed with a rake, not stung


before, so fearless. Paint the frantic
  confusion as she strikes at them;
paint the long lavender thread, unravelled
  in headlong flight, from her ripped hem;


paint her supporting blameless Abel
  through Eden spoilt; the mother-saint
forgiving the torn dress, applying
  the bluebag. Pain you cannot paint —

not then, not now, when pain assails you
  in matchless colours, burning bright,
erasing form, dissolving substance.
  You are the shade of its pure light.

When asked once, at an exhibition,
  "Do you believe in God?", for fun
you asked the questioner politely
  "The Blue God, or the Ginger One?"

When I heard this, the colours took me
  through half a lifetime to that day
when I believed the wasps had punished
  my sins in God's mysterious way,

probed my black mocking heart, and taught me
  the foolishness of unbelief.
Now it is pain that I believe in,
  saying at your side, like the Good Thief,

"Remember me." Remember talking
  late at night of the language game.
"The image of pain is not a picture,"
  said Wittgenstein, "is not the same

as anything we call a picture."
  Tell me, who can talk sense with pain
when it becomes the body's language,
  and its unpictured signs remain

a personal mystery affirming
  the person in whose breast reside
all deities, beyond games or language,
  the problem no one gets outside

to solve. With colours in solution
   fix me the opalescent light
of our lost years in solid pigment,
   build me art's heaven in hell's despite:

two children bathed in bluebag, sharing
   the softness of one earthly breast;
old Nobodaddy's social workers
   smoked without mercy from their nest;

picture the tiger-sun declining
   as memory lights with equal flame
vestiges of the pain that leads us
   to truth beyond the language game.


# Springtime, Oyster Cove

*To the memory of James McAuley*

Springtime returns, old love thought lost
and found by chance. The hillside lapses
from its strict tones of cold to sweetness.
Wildflowers illuminate their names:
white iris, scorpion everlasting,
lilac bells, speedwell, waxflower, musk.
Seabirds possess their field of blue,
songbirds their bowl of milky sky.
Sapphire, turquoise, pastoral
viridian on the hills of Bruny.
Everything's occupied with life,
thrusting, relentless, fountaining
with sap and hope.
                       You dreamed about
a world where all is possible, all

creatures teach wisdom to their young.
The serpent of the intellect,
redeemed, coils in majestic truth.
Children of men outname old Adam
in peaceful cities.
                        The sun sinks
ancient and great.
                        Set down the wine
among the living. Evening falls
in saffron, lilac, melting silver.
Death's soft tongue breaks your bones, in darkness
returns you to the earth you loved,
its changing lights more beautiful,
to those who mourn you, for your song.


# Evening, Oyster Cove

*What is history to me? Mine is the first and only world*
—Wittgenstein

The early painters had it right:
    closefisted gums, hills humped on hills,
chill distances where the heart might
    stop in its tracks for loneliness.

Calm tide. My solitary wake
    arrows the glistening waterskin.
Crows, bound for Bruny. Wingbeats make
    the sound of runners breathing, in

their firm compacted paths of air.
    Sunset pours golden syrup on
the northern sandstone. Treetops flare
    briefly, and then the sun is gone.

My geese call from the western rise —
    Babydoll, Fido, Stagolee —
the haunting wildness of their cries
    mocks well-fed domesticity.

This elbow of the shallow bay
    crooked an unchilded dying race
whose liquid language ebbed away.
    Shadows forgather in this place:

Jackey, Patty, Queen Caroline,
    Lalla Rookh — white contemptuous names
cloaked the heartsickness of decline.
    The Governor brought them children's games,

toys, marbles, balls. Let history write
    death after hopeless death. The sea's
a sheet of melancholy light.
    Herons half made of shadow seize

their meal, like necromancers search
    obscuring crystal for a sign.
My boat grounds gently on the beach.
    Home to books, fire and chilled white wine.

Ghosts of the night mist, set me free.
    Forgive, until the past is called
wisdom, and history can be
    told in some last redeeming world.

# A Memory of James McAuley

Vines, roses, espaliered almonds:
my comely Edwardian garden
disposed in the valley's fossil bed.
We were sitting with mugs of tea
and a shuffled *Quadrant* folder
among papery everlastings.
Pippins and plums were ripe.
That season the grapes would sweeten.

I had chipped from shrouding rock
a Devonian brachiopod
which you turned and turned in one hand,
musing
        "When this was newly made
the earth was already old,
but then, for the first time, clothed in green."
You spoke of great ferns uncoiling
their fiddle-scroll fronds in voiceless air.
"They gave us our atmosphere."
The fossil lay warm in your palm.
"A palaeozoic poem," (you were smiling)
"well made, with form and rhyme."

# "Let Sappho Have the Singing Head"

— Dorothy Hewett, *The Inheritors*

I   *Evensong*

A grotesque moon, waxing close,
it hovers late in twilight
raven dark, parrot green.
I say, who let you in?
I was listening to Caruso.
You smell of earth, I don't
want bloody conversation.

I turn the music off.
The Head declares itself:
    "Horrors and deeds of horror
    death from the world's beginning
    dreams known to all the living
    peaceful and wrathful gods
    drift of unhappy ghosts

    I change, singing whatever
    cannot be solved or changed."
I think of Mahler shouting
at his orchestra, TOO LOUD!
before a note was played.
Cool it, cool it, I say.
Sing this ordinary day.


II   *The Head Sings, to a Guitar*

Crazy baby, don't think I'm a doll
    you can kiss and throw down on the mat
like a child who knows nothing at all
    of loving and where it's at.

Don't think you can turn me over
    and hope I will sing *ma-ma*.
You've made a mistake, old lover.
    I'll tell you how things are

in words that will really astound you
    and scratch your self-esteem
while the suburbs twinkle around you
    and the ribs of water gleam

and nursemaid conscience assures you
    that bogies lurk in the yard
and crackling with virtue pours you
    the milk of self-regard.

In darkness I'll find your door
    and softly, softly come through
and bite your veins and pour
    my nightmares into you

and lie at your side unmoving
    while you scream and scream in the night.
It will be too late for loving
    when nurse comes with the light.

III   *Diotima*

I am curved, a shadow in crystal
and cannot break through to the world,
so reach for my one drug, music,
and turn it on. It's Caruso.
He is singing *M'appari*.

Well, let life imitate art.
A tenor sings, "Like a dream",
and a woman sits still and listens.

I feel the drug take hold
of my body, a lover's touch,

as I stare bemused at the fire
and hear the soft rustle of coals
orange hot from the heart of some tree
in a dialogue of passion
darkening, descending to charcoal.

And the scratched old record glows
with the fire of that marvellous voice
too dear for death's possessing.
For pain to exist in the world
there must be a creature to feel it.

Return: I will change you heads.
Have mine, it has no illusions
about being tried in the balance
of God and the suburbs and found
wanting. Take up this coal

still glowing, to set on your tongue.
Sing me the local swans
flying low over luminous water
and the usual crows in the west
croaking, to have the taste

in your mouth and know the wine gone:
that is the anguish of thirst.
Sing me the spectrum of pain
as I sit with your head for mine
steady and cool, not reaching

for the holy saving poison:
to dream my death. The half moon
like a slice of fruit newly cut

moves westward in frosty air.
My tongue has known you. The world

turns on to the shadow of night.
I watch the sparks fly upward,
the fire consuming itself.
There is music of former times
at our place of parting. I wait

as the soul might wait in the grave
through the body's decomposition
from dream to dream of a summer's day
with the half moon swinging westward
desire bleeding away.


# Mappings of the Plane

All those scales we rehearsed
on other instruments
useless. Our fingering
opened such intervals
and crazy fugues we were
live drunk with space. We scaled

each other. On our skins
the bloom of moisture. Given
the centre of reflection
we are glassed, an ordered pair.
Given our mad notation
we'll find a tune no air

can ruffle. Recombine
our elements. We are
real numbers, and perhaps
the solution is unique.
Reduced to the absurd
wrap ourselves in dry sheets.


    I am cooled to this transparency. Recharge me.
    Water, I give you leave to enter me,
    cold water blazing with a light of harvests.

    "It was a summer's day at harvest-time" —
    stories begin so. Cloudlight shone like glass
    in mild midwinter. All the leaves were still.

    Now let all those who drank with us remember
    how I was hung with earrings from the plane
    trees' numberless resource, "and thou beside me."

    Let those ill-tempered blades sent out to assault us
    slice through the inverse mappings of the plane
    at shadows. We preserve our distances.

    I am high on acid rock, on wandering glitter.
    Sunset lights the King's sails with mocking splendour.
    South and south the white sea-eagle hunts

    as if he feared his quarry gone for ever.
    His wingbeat gleams and vanishes in light.
    I am hungry, tearing oysters from the rocks

    My hands bleed, and I bathe them in the water
    which takes my blood to heart, and changes colour.
    Hölderlin, Nerval, Lenz, Novalis, Trakl,

night's actors gather close in darkening wings,
and reach for me: Isolde on the rocks.
But I am poured out for a drier throat.

We shall walk again by water under plane trees.
Sweet weather will recharge our cup of laughter,
the clattering weathercocks revolve with song.


Something more than wind moves in the leaves,
a new interpretation of their shade
where trees lace arms together. Something grieves:
autumnal breath whose perfect intonation
calls out of nothing all the sobbing airs.
Such ripeness, steady: golden ash still firm,
poplars abiding in their spires of light;
and sadness welling from the shades below.

> Leaves conjured off, you wait in sombre
> trunks, my desolate harlequins.
> Wind shakes your earrings without number.
> A council gardener begins
> to prune your wands. Black prophet crow
> flaps from the rustling drifts below
> to his old testament of air
> to pick himself a newborn eye.
> The clouds mass close like poodle hair,
> or lamb fleece, in a frozen sky.
> The heart's a carnival, the mind
> a cloudy mirror gone half blind.
>
> Let me be your golden child.
> Father Aether, lift me high,
> let the darkening gold of churches
> shade the souls for whom Christ died.

When the cataclysmic waters
wash towards chaos, let me be
your golden child aloft on discourse,
tell me what I long to hear:
that the tiger's bones shall mend,
and the mammoth finish eating
all his sweet Siberian grasses.
Let the arctic corals flourish,
let me be your golden child.
Take me past the bounds of silence.
Let me cross your ordered fields
rolling in the flowers of nonsense,
let me understand my dreams
through the language as it is.
Since the world and life are one,
let me be your golden child.


# Return of the Native

The big house is turned into flats, the last camphor laurel
cut down, alas; the street paved, the cool weatherboard suburb
gone trendy with fancy brick; but new roses spill
their old abundance of scent, and across the kerb

as if this were a film, a Mintie wrapper blows.
So cut to two freckled children unwrapping Minties
in their camphor laurel house, and from wide windows
let the sounds of teacups and voices and laughter rise.

It is late afternoon, and the towering cumulus gather
over city, suburb and treehouse as everyone tells
silly stories. A pause. A rich baritone voice is clear:
"Well, a gentleman knows where he is if the police
    own the brothels."

The grown-ups shriek, and repeat the curious line.
Heaven cracks open. The children run, drenched, inside,
and the girl, who learns like a parrot, repeats it again
and is slapped into tears without knowing how she has
   offended.

And Freddy, who said it while managing his tea
with his hand and his hook says, "She didn't understand,"
and talks about Little Pitchers and says he's sorry.
(He told me once: "When the Germans shot off my hand

God gave me this hook, it's much better for carrying parcels."
I believed the curving steel grew out of his arm.)
But it's time for some good old songs, and music quells
the world's injustice, and clears away the storm.

> My taxi is waiting. The driver puts down his book.
> It's Volume Two of the brick-red paperback Popper.
> I say, "Full Marx?" He grins, "Half. Have you had a
>    good look?
> Was that your old home? Do you like what they've
>    done to her?
>
> Do you like what they've done to this old State
>    of yours?
> I'm a useless M.A. It's no use whingeing, but.
> You can't sing hymns in the park, and the police own
>    the parlours.
> But I've a sick wife and a kid, so I keep my mouth
>    shut.
>
> Ban Uranium, one bald tyre, they'll have you off.
> If you're sporting a Jesus Saves they'll let you go
> without tyres or lights. You'd better go back down
>    south. "
> I remember Freddy singing "My old Shako",

    and would like to say, he'd given a hand for freedom
    and would use his hook if anyone threatened his rights.
    But the truth is, he'd have voted to build the Bomb
    and to clean the long-haired larrikins out of the streets.

Turn like a jewel that small clear scene in your head:
    cloud-blaze, leaf-glitter, loved faces, a radiant voice
    singing "Fifty years ago . . ." Though you summon the dead
    you cannot come as a child to your father's house.

# The Sharpness of Death

I

Leave me alone. — You will?
That's your way with us women.
You've left my mother so,
desolate in my father's house.
But that's not what I mean.
Suppose we come to terms:
you take one day for each
day that I've wished to die.
Give me more time for time
that was never long enough.
Look, here's a list of names.
Take these, the world will bless you.
Death, you've become obscene.
Nobody calls you *sweet* or *easeful* now.
You're in the hands of philosophers
who cut themselves, and bleed,
and know that knives are sharp,
but prove with complex logic
there's no such thing as sharpness.

## II

Heidegger

Like Wittgenstein, he found much cause to wonder
  "that there are things in being".
Searching for roots, he thought all words were names.
  Given the German language
and his training as a Jesuit seminarian
  he could talk about God's *Dasein*,
and in untranslatable reasonings maintain
  that the human concept *Being*
and the question "What is Being?" are essential:
  since man's a language user
he must say things *are*, or cannot speak at all.
  He called philosophy,
in his late works, "the enemy of thinking".
  Rilke said song was Dasein.
Heidegger left ontology for Hölderlin
  and his blessed Grecian world,
"the language in which Being speaks to us".
  Untranslatable as ever!
Was it significant nonsense or deep insight
  flowed from his pen? He thought
much about dying. No one could die for him.
  Poetry led him
close to the Logos. Nothing could be proved,
  but much was hinted.
Death, he said, was "the ultimate situation".
  I hope he found some light
beyond that field of black everlasting flowers.

III

Nasturtiums

Purest of colours, how they shone
while we talked in your studio.
Light like a noble visitor
stayed with us briefly and moved on.
A schoolgirl bringing flowers, an artist
accepting colour and crazy love,
we stand among the plaster mouldings
of figures from an earlier time.
How would you ever know me now
if I came to your grave and called you,
unless I brought those flowers, those colours,
that ray of light descending through
the room's eccentric fenestration?
Seed of the seed of countless seasons
blossoms to hold the light that's gone.

IV

Death, I will tell you now:
my love and I stood still
in the roofless chapel. My
body was full of him, my
tongue sang with his juices, I
grew ripe in his blond light.
If I fall from that time,
then set your teeth in me.

# Three Poems for Margaret Diesendorf

I  *Sparrows*

Matthew says two for a farthing,
and Luke, five for two farthings —
neatly threaded on skewers,
housewives shopping around:
"They're cheaper down the road."

Why does he let them fall
if he loves the world at all?

We've hundreds here. They come
and go all day unharmed.
They feed beside my geese,
while the lark who starts up singing
feeds himself as he will.

As the psalmist says, I watch
like a sparrow on the roof.
Many I loved are gone.
Death has them in his net.
The God of Israel let
the fowler's snare enclose them.

Sparrows flock to my pond.
One, on a lily leaf,
twitters and drinks. I'm charmed.

Nothing can correspond
to my wonder at the world.

II  *Towards a Meeting*

I had an image of you: a bird
between continent and continent
with foreign songs in your head
through lightning, rainbow, cloud

beating down the northern stars
forgotten lights on cruel waters
through snow, wind, darkness, rain,
with your one possession: song.

And I saw you once in a strange dream
where I walked through intricate gates of iron
and asked you to translate
*Gruppe aus dem Tartarus*.

Now I have your picture in my hand.
In a summer photograph you stand
in a gallery of flowers.
Colours sing in your dress.

Who knows when it will come to pass —
we'll meet by happy circumstance
and talk, in a real room,
through image, picture, dream.


III  *Memento*

Those delicate pressed flowers you send
like gentle prayers from friend for friend
lie pressed in favourite books again:
Robert Penn Warren, *Wittgenstein's
Vienna, The Unquiet Grave*.

Here's one, imperial purple still,
fine-veined in darkness. (Alt Wien!
Wittgenstein with his troubled brilliance
stalking the shadows of the Prater
to some unphilosophic end.)

Down under my old Funk & Wagnall
and Gardiner's Egyptian Grammar
lie *Tetratheca glandulosa*
and *Helichrysum scorpioides,*
lilac bells, scorpion everlasting,
feeling the weight of common names,
gathered from my dry, stony hillside
in spring when James McAuley died.

But for you, I'll press a Running Postman,
symbol of your enchanting letters.
The mind falls open on the past:
    Jim's wineglass set on my piano
    as he sight-reads through a book of lieder.
    He tries "The Lion's Bride", by Schumann.
    At the moment when the lovecrazed lion
    begins to crunch the keeper's daughter
    in her bridegroom's presence, the translator
    makes the youth, calling for a weapon,
    ineptly cry, "Give me an arm!"
    Jim roars and chokes and waves his wineglass,
    leonine, overwhelmed by laughter.

He told me once that your translations
let the light of another language
shine through his poems "as through clear glass".
In his memory, I offer this.

# A Quartet for Dorothy Hewett

I   *Twilight*

Twilight. Field-mouse light. They rustle
in shadowy palaces of hay.
My old cat, Mr Gabriel Fur,
would hunt to keep the mice away
and like a Harlem Globetrotter
juggle his prizes in the air.

Let the mice fear the owl's soft rush
now their lithe enemy is gone
to nourish a viburnum bush.
On his last night on earth he came
to grizzle gently at my door,
then lay beside me, fur to skin.

Did he recall who killed Cock Robin
when we rose up to earliest birdsong?
"We do not live to experience death,"
said my favourite philosopher
(thinking perhaps about his own).
Tell me what I experience, then,

when I wake to open the house door
hearing a cry I cannot hear,
or when I walk in the scythed field
watching the world give up its light,
and feel ghost-footed at my back
a presence in the rustling stack.

## II  *Goose-girl*

Darkness my refuge, sleep my consolation
hold me a moment on the crest of sunrise.
Out of the false lucidity of dreams I
   know myself waking.

Now I will walk as if you were beside me
hearing the birds' ancestral incantations.
Light turns familiar landscape to a spectral
   anguish of strangeness.

We were like princes choosing their disguises,
meeting at last in joyful recognition,
laughing unmasked at life, the royal game, whose
   rules are all fatal.

Mantled in snow my white, my grey geese nested.
Now they walk safely with their golden children
knowing the hand that feeds them is immortal:
   I am their goddess.

Where are you now, who came through dream and darkness
bodied in light, whom light dissolves to absence?
How will you know me, barefoot in the pasture,
   dressed as a goose-girl?

Under the poem of words there shines another,
like a gold flagon arrogantly buried
by one who knows that earth itself will yield it
   to the true lover.

III  *A Simple Story*

A visiting conductor
    when I was seventeen,
took me back to his hotel room
    to cover the music scene.

I'd written a composition.
    Would wonders never cease —
here was a real musician
    prepared to hold my piece.

He spread my score on the counterpane
    with classic casualness,
and put one hand on the manuscript
    and the other down my dress.

It was hot as hell in The Windsor.
    I said I'd like a drink.
We talked across gin and grapefruit,
    and I heard the ice go clink

as I gazed at the lofty forehead
    of one who led the band,
and guessed at the hoarded sorrows
    no wife could understand.

I dreamed of a soaring passion
    as an egg might dream of flight,
while he read my crude sonata.
    If he'd said, "That bar's not right,"

or, "Have you thought of a coda?"
    or, "Watch that first repeat,"
or, "Modulate to the dominant,"
    he'd have had me at his feet.

But he shuffled it all together,
    and said, "That's *lovely*, dear,"
as he put it down on the washstand
    in a way that made it clear

that I was no composer.
    And I being young and vain,
removed my lovely body
    from one who'd scorned my brain.

I swept off like Miss Virtue
    down dusty Roma Street,
and heard the goods trains whistle
    WHO? WHOOOOOO? in aching heat.


IV   *Dorothy, Reading in Hobart*

Lustrous angel, who, if I cried, would hear me,
I call you woman, goddess, muse.
In your dress like the blue between clouds
come out of Tartarus singing
the worst of truth in your voice of shadow.

Truth is humbling. Truth is the last tram
you have to catch, and strap-hang, or not get home.
Truth is the watchman running to King David
with news to weep at, words to tighten harpstrings
like plucked hair. Truth's a court for owls,
a motel room where nymphs and satyrs
howl for nembutal, reclining
in odd conjunction, now-and-never
coupling their life sentences.
Truth will dash out our teeth.

Sing the love-letters never posted,
the lovely game where art is wasted.
Voice of lustre, voice of shadow,
sing the brightness turned to sadness,
death of the suburbs, death of habit,
spirits bowed in milky sweetness,
sing Tennysonian afternoons
when history sighed and harvests parted
over most unhappy shades.

A woman still as a Dutch painting
takes her pen, the old-gold light
cracks itself to mirror-splinters.

Charm with your haunting vox humana
Merlin from his malign enchantment.
Melt the black frost, mysterious angel.
Heaven's long emptied of its gods.
Fill the void with a woman's voice.

# The Secret Life of Frogs

Mr Gabriel Fur, my Siamese,
brings to the hearth a Common Toadlet,
*Crinia tasmaniensis*.
Mice are permitted, frogs forbidden.
It will live. I carry it outside.
Its heartbeat troubles my warm hand
and as I set it down I see
two small girls in a warmer land.

> My friend Alice and I would sit
> cradling our frogs behind the tankstand.

Other fathers would talk about
the Great War. Mine would only say,
"I used to be a stretcher-bearer."
Not seen, not heard, in childhood's earshot
of the women on the back veranda,
we knew about atrocities.
Some syllables we used as charms:
Passchendaele  Mons  Gallipoli.
We knew about Poor George, who cried
if any woman touched her hair.
He'd been inside a brothel when
the Jerries came and started shooting.
(We thought a brothel was a French
hotel that served hot broth to diggers.)
The girl that he'd been with was scalped.
Every Frog in the house was killed.

Well, that was life for frogs. At school
the big boys blew them up and spiked them.
One bully had the very knife
with which his father killed ten Germans —
twenty — a hundred — numbers blossomed.
Dad the Impaler! making work
for the more humble stretcher-bearers.

In safety by the dripping tankstand
our frogs with matchstick hands as pale
as the violet stems they lived among
cuddled their vulnerable bellies
in hands that would not do them wrong.

# Space of a Dream

For the first time since your death
I see you alive in a dream
in your body's early beauty,
your hair angel-yellow, your lips
set firm in the fullness of youth.
You are sitting with folded hands
in the dining-room of my old house
waiting for a good meal
in shadowy green wine-flagon light.

Our friend is with us. He walks outside
among ragged fire-shaped flowers.
Something is stuck in his skull:
a metal sharkfin? — a piece of sword.

The meal is ready. I set out bread,
wineglasses, grilled spring lamb chops.
Our friend begins to eat and drink.
Juices flow from the rose-brown meat.
As he bends his head I see
it was only a crest of hair
that shone in his skull like a sword.

You stare at us without speaking
across your untasted meal.
Small golden words fly out
like bees from your lion's body
and shine in a soundless phrase of light:
> *Untouched by human hand*.

It is meant as a joke, and you smile.
At the edge of sleep I know
that you cannot eat with the living.
From the alien space of a dream
without history or intention
I am thrust into actual sunlight
from level to level of thought
and symbol. I know this dream
for what it is: the beginning of healing.
You stiffen to legend
Tristan
        the heart's endless need.


# Mother Who Gave Me Life

Mother who gave me life
I think of women bearing
women. Forgive me the wisdom
I would not learn from you.

It is not for my children I walk
on earth in the light of the living.
It is for you, for the wild
daughters becoming women,

anguish of seasons burning
backward in time to those other
bodies, your mother, and hers
and beyond, speech growing stranger

on thresholds of ice, rock, fire,
bones changing, heads inclining
to monkey bosom, lemur breast,
guileless milk of the word.

I prayed you would live to see
Halley's Comet a second time.
The Sister said, When she died
she was folding a little towel.

You left the world so, having lived
nearly thirty thousand days:
a fabric of marvels folded
down to a little space.

At our last meeting I closed
the ward door of heavy glass
between us, and saw your face
crumple, fine threadbare linen

worn, still good to the last,
then, somehow, smooth to a smile
so I should not see your tears.
Anguish: remembered hours:

a lamp on embroidered linen,
my supper set out, your voice
calling me in as darkness
falls on my father's house.

from *Bone Scan* (1988)

# Class of 1927

*Slate*

Quite often in some trendy quarter
the passion to redecorate
those areas concerned with water
results in an expanse of slate.
Cork tiling's warmer, vinyl's neater.
Slate's forty dollars a square metre.
In kitchen, laundry, loo, I see
the stuff the State School gave us free,
and very soon my morbid, chronic
nostalgia swells to recreate
slate-pencil's piercing squeal on slate,
beloved of all those bored demonic
infants whose purpose was to make
mischief purely for mischief's sake.

We sat, ranked by examination,
those with the best marks at the back.
In undisguised discrimination
at the front sat the dim, the slack,
where they could not converse or fiddle;
and in the undistinguished middle
the hard triers, the fairly bright
laboured to get their set work right
not out of any love of study
but simply to escape the cane.
Somehow the teacher knew whose brain
was cleared by stirring, whose was muddy.
One vacant lad, condemned to go
from year to year in the front row,

was said to have three skulls, poor creature.
Everyone liked to feel his head
and demonstrate its curious feature:
ridge after ridge of bone instead
of brain. Bonehead was oddly charming.
His eagerness was so disarming
the whole class used him as a pet
though he was likely to forget
between instruction and retrieval
the object he was sent to find.
No angst stirred his unleavened mind.
He beamed, and hummed, and knew no evil.
The doctor's son, a clever skite,
found inexpressible delight

in cruelty. This boy collected,
or stole, unpleasant instruments;
with these, at playtime, he dissected
lizards and frogs, or spiked their vents
to see how long they took in dying.
One day the class, kept in for sighing
when Sir set homework, heard a squeak.
Being on our honour not to speak
while Sir was briefly absent (bearing
his cane as always) we turned round
and witnessed, as the source of sound,
a captive mouse, its torturer swearing
because the victim tried to bite.
The back row, silent out of fright,

did nothing, and the middle section
saw, but pretended not to look.
Bonehead, after a brief inspection,
stopped smiling; turned again and took
his slate out of its slot; descended
in fury, and with one blow ended

the wanton vivisector's sport.
Then revolution of a sort
broke out. The stricken head was gory.
We stamped and cheered our hero on.
The unhappy mouse was too far gone
to benefit from Bonehead's glory,
or squeak for victory, or curse
the arrangement of this universe.

When Sir returned the class was sitting
so quietly he racked his wits
and stroked his cane and walked round hitting
his leg, but didn't find the bits
of slate we hid in hasty cleaning.
Nor did he grasp the hidden meaning
of some congealing drops of red.
"Where did you get that bloody head?"
"Knocked it." "Go home. That cut needs dressing."
Our golden silence filled the room.
We sat preparing to resume
our work as if it were a blessing
to write on slate, for Sir to see,
the conjugation of *to be*.


*The Spelling Prize*

*Every Child's Book of Animal Stories.*
To compete, we stood on the wooden forms
that seated four in discomfort.
When you missed your word, you sat down
and wrote it out twenty times.
At last only two were left:
Ella and I, who had sailed
past *ghost, nymph, scheme, flight, nephew,*
the shoals of o - u - g - h

and i before e, stood waiting
for the final word. Whoever
put her hand up first when Sir
announced it, could try to spell it.
A pause, while Sir went outside.
Some of the girls started hissing,
"Give Ella a chance. Let her win."

Through the window I saw the playground
bare as a fowlyard, the ditch
in a paddock beyond where frogs
lived out whatever their life was
before the big boys impaled them
on wooden skewers, a glint
from a roof in the middle distance
that was Ella's home. I had been there

the week before, when my grandmother went
to take their baby, the ninth,
my brother's old shawl. Ella coaxed me
to a ramshackle tinroofed shed
where her father was killing a bull calf.
A velvety fan of blood
opened out on the concrete floor
as one of her brothers pumped the forelegs:
"You do this to empty the heart."

The father severed the head, and set it
aside on a bench where the eyes, still trusting,
looked back at what had become
of the world. It was not the sight
of the entrails, the deepening crimson
of blood that sent me crying
across the yard, but the calf's eyes watching
knife, whetstone, carcase, the hand that fed.

Ella followed. "I'll show you my toys."
In that house where nobody owned
a corner, a space they might call their own,
she kept two old dolls in a shoebox.
Below me the whispers continued:
"Let Ella win the prize."
Why, now, does memory brood
on Sir's return, and the moment

when he put down his cane and smoothed
his hair grease-tight on his skull
and snapped out the last word: MYSTIC,
a word never found in our Readers.
My innocent hand flew up.
Sheer reflex, but still, I knew it,
and knew I could slip in a k
or an i for a y and lose,

but did not, and sixty years
can't change it; I stand in the playground
and the pale dust stirs as my friends
of the hour before yell "Skite!"
and "Showoff!" and "Think you're clever!"
They gather round Ella, who turns
one hurt look from her red-rimmed eyes
at my coveted, worthless prize.


*Religious Instruction*

The clergy came in once a week for Religious Instruction.
Divided by faith, not age, we were bidden to be,
(except for the Micks and a Jew) by some curious deduction
Presbyterian, Methodist, Baptist or C of E.

The Micks were allowed to be useful, to tidy the playground.
But Micah, invited to join them, told Sir "They'd only
give me a hiding", and stayed inside; moved round
as he chose with his book of Hebrew letters, a lonely

example, among the tender lambs of Jesus,
of good behaviour. Handsome as a dark angel
he studied while the big boys laboured to tease us
with hair-tweak, nib-prick, Chinese burns, as the well

of boredom overflowed in games of noughts
and crosses, spitballs, and drawings so obscene
if Sir had found them they'd have earned us six cuts.
"You give me real insight into original sin,"

said one minister in despair, intercepting some verses
describing him as Old Swivelneck. Beaked like a sparrowhawk
he clawed at his collar and singled me out from his class.
I feared his anger rightly, feared he would talk

to our headmaster, or Sir. I stood in disgrace.
Then a quiet voice from the back interrupted his wrath:
"*I am ready to forgive.*" "Who said that? Stand up in your
   place! "
Micah stood. "It was said by the Lord God of Sabaoth."

Then we heard the monitor's footsteps. Saved by the bell!
In a tumult of voices we spilled into sunlight to play,
a host of rejoicing sinners, too young to feel
original darkness under that burning day.

*The Twins*

Three years old when their mother died
in what my grandmother called
accouchement, my father labour,
they heard the neighbours intone
"A mercy the child went with her."

Their father raised them somehow.
No one could tell them apart.
At seven they sat in school
in their rightful place, at the top
of the class, the first to respond
with raised arm and finger-flick.

When one gave the answer, her sister
repeated it under her breath.
An inspector accused them of cheating,
but later, in front of the class,
declared himself sorry, and taught us
a marvellous word: *telepathic*.

On Fridays, the story went,
they slept in the shed, barred in
from their father's rage as he drank
his dead wife back to his house.
For the rest of the week he was sober
and proud. My grandmother gave them
a basket of fruit. He returned it.
"We manage. We don't need help."

They could wash their own hair, skin rabbits,
milk the cow, make porridge, clean boots.

Unlike most of the class I had shoes,
clean handkerchiefs, ribbons, a toothbrush.

We all shared the schoolsores and nits
and the language I learned to forget
at the gate of my welcoming home.

One day as I sat on the fence
my pinafore goffered, my hair
still crisp from the curlers, the twins
came by. I scuttled away
so I should not have to share
my Saturday sweets. My mother
saw me, and slapped me, and offered
the bag to the twins, who replied
one aloud and one sotto voce,
"No thank you. We don't like lollies."

They lied in their greenish teeth
as they knew, and we knew.
                              Good angel
give me that morning again
and let me share, and spare me
the shame of my parents' rebuke.

If there are multiple worlds
then let there be one with an ending
quite other than theirs: leaving school
too early and coming to grief.

Or if this is our one life sentence,
hold them in innocence, writing
*Our Father which art in Heaven*
in copperplate, or drawing
(their work being done) the same picture
on the backs of their slates: a foursquare
house where a smiling woman
winged like an angel welcomes
two children home from school.

# Bone Scan

*Thou hast searched me and known me. Thou knowest my
downsitting and mine uprising*
— Psalm 139

In the twinkling of an eye,
in a moment, all is changed:
on a small radiant screen
(honeydew melon green)
are my scintillating bones.
Still in my flesh I see
the God who goes with me
glowing with radioactive
isotopes. This is what he
at last allows a mortal
eye to behold: the grand
supporting frame complete
(but for the wisdom teeth),
the friend who lives beneath
appearances, alive
with light. Each glittering bone
assures me: you are known.


# The Night Watch

I am lying like a creature
from outer space, equipped
for sound and colour vision,
in a capsule of discomfort.
Tubes issue from my body,
one taking, one receiving.

Here and there a window
in the hospital, the space ship,
glows and returns to blankness.
The night crew keep their stations.
Who can make sense of pain
with stars and clouds obscured

in a near-but-never darkness:
the backsides of old buildings
and the Savings Bank sign turning,
symbol of some bizarre
religion of this planet —
Invest and find salvation.

Save and be saved. No use
to me, I can save nothing.
Only watch, in my sleepless
journey towards a grounding
I dare not think about,
the neon sign revolving.

I know a bank . . . where
the wild thyme grows . . . indeed
time has grown wild and warped
near the black hole of oblivion:
mind beaten, body showing
its true colours to strangers.

O that tongue of cadmium red
in one of Miro's paintings!
*Salveo*, I am well.
*Salvus*, well, sound, unharmed,
entire, whole, safe, uninjured.
And *salvia*, scarlet sage —

what sage would lie here playing
intellectual variations
for a night, a thousand hours,
on a single neon sign.
Here there's no price on heroes.
Better to ring for sleep.

So the mercy of a needle
brings me to a rough landing:
the rubbish men are loading
unspeakable detritus,
crashing with cheerful shouts
through a freezing mortal morning.

And the bank, no doubt for reasons
of economy, has turned
its symbol off. The crescent
moon and the morning star
over the Lands Department
fade into greater light.


## *I.M.* Philip Larkin

Sorrow will keep its hour
surpassing all belief.
It will push through pavements, open
when it means to. It will fall
as acid rain corroding
bell-throats. Sorrow will slide
down gutters of fine print.
At dusk, a rushing whiteness
will seize and hold you safe.

# Divertimento

*To Jan Sedivka*

I  *Notturno*

    Late-night music: frogs' irregular rhythm,
    bubble-recitative across the hill.
"All's well in well and waterhole, all's well
in wells and ponds and water's secret places.
Before Abraham, *we are*. Our frog-fugue sounded
while constellations changed, scale became feather,
earth heard, beyond our nocturne, human voices.
O we came up into the land of Egypt
countless, in kneading-troughs, in the King's chambers,
calling as we do now and shall again.
We'll croak our miracles when all kings are gone."

    They hear my crackling footfall, and fall silent,
    fellow by answering fellow on the hill.
    Ice light of the aurora veils Canopus:
    beauty like heartbreak, earth and time as still
    as if some unseen player, with a flute,
    ready to draw, but not yet drawing breath,
    had heard and memorized night's ancient airs.
    Only a flute could summon that pure music
    and fit our human breath to shimmering space.
    Not this frog-jollity that leaps again
    resonant, overlapping, ringing the changes.
    Our first music, perhaps; in long cave-watches
    when firelight died, frog-babble stayed to cheer us.
"The world's safe, if we bubble until dawn."

## II  *Affetuoso*

Picture a Brisbane afternoon
about half a century ago,
the air refreshed by sudden rain.
From our old house in Auchenflower
we see the City Hall's fine tower
unrivalled on the low skyline.

Mango, poinsettia, camphor laurel
throw shadows on our wide verandas.
Someone's arranged A Musical.
My mother's rounded up the faithful.
Staunch helpers bustle in the kitchen.
My task is to collect a florin

in my brass bowl from every guest
for the Widows and Orphans Christmas Feast.
I come to Mrs Nibbs, notorious
for make-up: pinky-lilac powder
and orange lips. I think she's glorious
and long to paint myself like her,

black eyebrows, lacquered hair and all.
I stand jiggling my begging-bowl.
She sneers, "You ignorant little girl!
I'm singing, so I needn't pay!"
I blush with shame. The programme starts,
Auchenflower's tribute to the arts:

I'll sing thee songs of Araby.
Thank God for a Garden. Soul of Mine.
O Dry Those Tears. Mountains o' Mourne.
Homing. Roses of Picardy.
Melisande in the Wood. Because.
Slave Song. Like to the Damask Rose.

Afternoon tea at last! So many
sandwiches, pikelets, airy sponges.
A woman says to Mrs Nibbs,
"While you were singing Soul of Mine,
my dear, I thought of Tetrazzini —
that tone like an old violin —

you know — a Stradivarius —"
My mother, passing with a dish
of cakes, too innocently says,
"I think the secret's in the varnish."
>    If some miraculous cassette
>    could recreate from memory's light
>
>    those singers and their music made
>    in unrecorded happiness;
>    restore the after-rain release
>    of flower-scent, leaf shine, cumulus glow,
>    what child in camphor-laurel shade
>    would bid me welcome long ago?

III  *Scherzo*

Look up at the moon
  sweeping out of her cloud
    like a full-bosomed singer
      preparing to lay us
        completely besotted
          with love in the aisles.

She's a sphere of old rock
  without means of support.
    What keeps her aloft
      in her silver-gilt halo?
        It's music that holds her
          securely in space.

So listen my darling
  come here in the shadow
    I swear if you kiss me
      we'll capture in concert
        the crystalline music
          that keeps her in place.


IV  *Postlude: Listening to Bach*

We owe our thanks to that philosopher,
Pythagoras of the theorem, for asserting
the geometry of music, its reflection
of the deep structural elements of the world.
   Sometimes an old dog by the fireside
   sleeping soundly through music, sighs and shivers;
   comes closer to be fondled, as if saying
   "I heard *something* — O let me understand
   what separates my speechless world from yours."
   Or howls, drawing in breath as if determined
   to echo something ancient and enduring,
   if talked about, unknown; if known, unspoken.

What figures Bach, enchanting architect,
conjures from air to bridge the cryptic spaces
between us and the peace-giving solution
to what our nature is, how the world's made;
what tunes to show, through all our imperfection,
that our familiar world is of one substance
with music nobly written, rightly played.

# Visitor

What light beguiles our dreams?
Does it keep Einsteinian laws?
How did your ashes seize
light, form, a speaking voice?

Are you ready now for my dream
in birdsong, lessening darkness?
Too late: you should have come
as once you came at midnight:

three days your newborn death
crazed me with nightmare howling.
You touched me. "I am come
from the grave to comfort you."

I slept in consolation
deeper than any sorrow.
Half-waking at my window
I rub my eyes, and see

a shadow cast by dreamlight
reflected in still water.
A heron stands unmoving,
a real bird on the rim

of an actual pond, possessing
somehow the selfsame space
(so music fills the body)
as your image in the dream.

You stare in ash-grey light,
pure dream of purer shadow,
then lift away, your voice
hungry and harsh.
                    All day

motions of thought are shaped
by curving wing, strict feather,
windstroke on ribs of water,
deathmask of clouded sky.

Which bird among the many
waiting stone-quiet with hunger
in leaden shallows came
to the threshold of my dream?

# Driving Home

*To the memory of Vera Cottew*

Stones, I think. They rise, crying.
Plover. One cloudy afternoon,
looking for mushrooms, we discovered
a plover's nest. "See how these eggs
marry colours of earth and stone."

Homeward in your old Baby Austin;
a mottled sky. You talked of Ruskin
finding in clouds a deep, calm presence
"which must be sought ere it is seen
and loved ere it is understood."

Passing a shabby country town you said,
"I love these lonely places
waiting for someone to be born
who'll make them great — but then they'll lose
their fields and plovers' eggs and mushrooms."

Miles. Years. This later landscape streaming
through earlier eyesight. You remain
somewhere in the confused arcades
of memory and longing, talking
of light and colour, bird and stone,

"St Mark's porches so full of doves" —
(Ruskin again) — "that living plume
and marble foliage seemed to mingle."
Come from the shades to comfort me!
You do, as I switch on the headlights,

though not as I expect. As often
in life you charmed me with surprises,
you draw out from my memory bank
a Brisbane City Hall recital:
an earnest pianist playing Bach.

The silvertails are bored. You nudge me,
flick your eyes upward: on the cornice
running right round the hall, a rat
has found himself without an exit.
Head after head begins to turn

and follow his demented circuit
round the ornamental ledge. It seems
he has to run when he hears music.
Between one item and another
he stops to rest and preen his whiskers.

Nobody listens to a note.
But oh, the applause! The pianist looks
bemused. We dry our tears of laughter.
Slowly, alert for dazzled creatures
on the dusty road, I reach my gate.

Presence not understood, but sought
and loved, remain with me tonight.


# The Sun Descending

*To the memory of Vera Cottew*

I have the Oxford Blake you left me;
hold it as if to bring you close.
Walk with me where the old houses
offer their frogs and gnomes and artless
flower-filled swans made of bald tyres.
It will soon be night. The gutter's pouring
quicksilver and a broken bottle
glitters like Cinderella's slipper.

You loved the first of everything:
first breath of any season, first
light on anything, first blossom
on any bush, brush-stroke on canvas.

Half a lifetime, and I am holding
your favourite book, dark blue and gold.
Your spirit brushes mine. You walk
under the shining heavenly shell
with me, clean through the solid world.

# Crow-Call

*He lives eternally who lives in the present*
—Wittgenstein, *Tractatus* 6.4311

Let this be eternal life:
light ebbing, my dinghy drifting
on watershine, dead centre
of cloud and cloud-reflection —
high vapour, mind's illusion.

And for music, Baron Corvo,
my half-tame forest raven
with his bad leg unretracted
beating for home, lamenting
or, possibly, rejoicing
that he saw the world at all.

Space of a crow-call, enclosing
the self and all it remembers.
Heart-beat, wing-beat, a moment.
My line jerks taut. The cod
are biting. This too is eternal:
the death of cod at twilight.
And this: food on my table
keeping a tang of ocean.

So many, in raven darkness.
Why give death fancy names?

Corvo, where have you settled
your crippled leg for the night?

# Sheba

Small saffron-tinted tabby
suffered, given a name:
Sheba. Sleek graduate from
our compost heap to home
comforts, you bring your own
gifts: bent mice, a ginger
tom kitten I put down.
Dark bands like ebony
bracelets adorn your limbs.

Companion of insomniac hours
now Mr Fur is gone,
you roll under the moon.
Latecomers. We are all
latecomers. As Hobbes said,
Hell is truth learned too late.
Learned late, in the small hours of dread
when light I thought would shine for ever
flows backward to the dead;
mice whisper, bring forth mice
to shred old cards and letters,
and the self I grew to fit
words that transformed the world
hears rock and water speak
in some forgotten language,
lapsing, lapsing, and fields
are full of gentle creatures
grazing towards their own slaughter.

Sheba leaps from her moth-waltzes
in spring grasses, sits and tunes
night to her piercing oboe voice:
> "Give me all my desire,
> moonlight and mice and milk,
> fancy food from your store.
> Cedar and sycamore
> flourish. Your roof is silver.
> Rejoice, and live for ever."

# A Feline Requiem

Tiglath-Pileser, named
for the grand Assyrian kings,
you came to us and claimed
the best chair in the house
at once, and like the Queen
of Sheba I brought tribute:
pilchards in aspic, mackerel
platter, things in creamed
gravy. Fur to the blazing
eyeballs you ruled the roost
of birds who sing in Pine Street.
Death lays his icy hand
on kings of any kind.
Now yours is the first grave
in our new arcadian grove.
It will be as beautiful
as old Anacreon's.
Thank God I had the means
to spare you a grim winter.

Your shroud's a hessian bag,
your own, in which you came
scolding from Middleton
on the long road to town.
We outlive so many loves.
In shade a royal presence
watches the sunlit lawn
and the unsuspecting doves.


## Schrödinger's Cat Preaches to the Mice

*To A.D. Hope*

Silk-whispering of knife on stone,
due sacrifice, and my meat came.
Caressing whispers, then my own
choice among laps by leaping flame.

What shape is space? Space will put on
the shape of any cat. Know this:
my servant Schrödinger is gone
before me to prepare a place.

So worship me, the Chosen One
in the great thought-experiment.
As in a grave I will lie down
and wait for the Divine Event.

The lid will close. I will retire
from sight, curl up and say Amen
to geiger counter, amplifier,
and a cylinder of HCN.

When will the geiger counter feel
decay, its pulse be amplified
to a current that removes the seal
from the cylinder of cyanide?

Dead or alive? The case defies
all questions. Let the lid be locked.
Truth, from your little beady eyes,
is hidden. I will not be mocked.

Quantum mechanics has no place
for what's there without observation.
Classical physics cannot trace
spontaneous disintegration.

If the box holds a living cat
no scientist on earth can tell.
But I'll be waiting, sleek and fat.
Verily, all will not be well

if, to the peril of your souls,
you think me gone. Know that this house
is mine, that kittens by mouse-holes
wait, who have never seen a mouse.

# Litany

*To the memory of Graeme Buchanan*

I

Insomnia's world: pale stars knotted together
like the back of someone's careless sewing, moonlight
(that safe and general antidote to reason)
masking ghosts who seen by day are only

rocks and young trees.
                    Who made it all? Who cares?
Perhaps the dead frame their impassioned sampler
the right way round: A Life, stitched with true meaning.


II

Rise up and walk, old friend, old body
longing for sleep, rise up and walk
while you have time on earth to follow
a moonlit road. The Channel lapses
to silence between winds and tides.
Lapwing, possum: familiar voices;
and in shadow, ancient presences
dreaming themselves young, naked, lean.
Who knows now where the graves are hidden?
Time's not another kind of distance.
More than a century of seasons —
and sorrow still so absolute
night cannot find a grief to match it.


III

The usual pre-dawn racket:
my roosters' craze for gold
brings fortune to the hills of Bruny.
Frieze from a Theban tomb:
profile, blank eye, heraldic posture,
they stare me out. They know
one of them's for the Grim Reaper.
He'll not wheeze and forgive.
He'll fight, and go down raging.
Look where his brother scarred my wrist
in permanent revenge.

There's an old Bulgarian proverb:
Whatever is, is somehow.
There's your Heidegger in a nutshell!
You shall not all die, my gilded boys.
One of my children dreamed
of a fowl who came to dinner saying
"Nothing nicer than roast person."
Some of you will be changed
to person. We must live together,
feasting and feasted-on, somehow.
Somehow.


IV

Bracken still clenched, and Running Postman
hardly afoot, but somewhere, close
to its appointed time, the love vine
will keep its word.
                       I find its promised
garland of blue in tangled heath,
forceful and delicate. Words fail,
often, but earth will not forsake us,
will hold us fast.
                       I need no more,
can bear no more today, so bind
this wreath of comfort round my wrist.

## V

*Ruh'n in Frieden, alle Seelen*

I heard you play this once for a young singer
who could not quite encompass Schubert's phrases,
yet only those who knew the song could tell
how you lifted her beyond the limitations

of her imperfect skill, drew us all closer
together in the music. Take your rest
beloved musician, teacher, friend, whose gifts
are carried, life to life, by many hands.


# Night and Dreams

### I

"I come to you in a dream of ages
past," sings Crab. He swirls his velvet-
seaweed cloak. "When first we met,
and last, you will recall, I was
imprisoned in your father's house."

Sea colours on his carapace,
wave-hiss, tide-rustle in his voice.
"Some fiend had tied my fearful claws —"
—Yes, I recall. I must have been
a skinny child of eight or nine

that night my father brought you home —
"No, let *me* tell," says Crab, "this is
*my* aria, *my* party piece.

Grandmother, mother, father, brother
and you, went to the local theatre

leaving me bound in parching darkness.
I prayed: Redeemer Crab, release me
by your own sidelong righteousness
from these straightforward evildoers.
Take me where my transparent children

float in their manifold sea vision.
Silence. Mouse-whisper, cockroach-scuffle.
I felt, not far, the Brisbane River
ebbing to salt creek, mangrove swamp,
and burst my bonds, O yes I did!

and raged through your dark house, and hid.
That night you dared not go to bed
finding me gone when you returned.
Splintered pencils and toys proclaimed
my ocean strength. How soon forgotten

what Stan and Olly did and said!
Time, time. I felt the tide returning
far off. O Salt Redeemer, come
(I prayed) let navies drown to feed me
with rotten stump, decaying belly,

or if I am to die, allow me
one crunchbone tender-balancing foot."
— My father caught you. "Ah, he did.
'We'll cook the brute tonight,' he said.
'Bring me the hatpin.' Someone put

a diamond eye on a steel stalk
into your father's hand to stab

my stalked eyes. O the blaze of pain
eclipsing light's immense mandala!
Seagreen, seablue, I raged to red.

Boiling, crab died. I became Crab."


## II

Crab is dressed for the feast: on lettuce shredded
to seaweed ribbons, cracked claws reassembled,
he lies among parsley curls and radish roses.
Our starchy Sunday-snowy cloth is set
with what remains of Greatgrandmother's china,
translucent white, rimmed with a deepsea blue.
On his great serving dish Crab's at the centre
of a splendid colour wheel: cucumber slices,
tomato, celery, carrot, egg: my work,
duly admired. My grandmother says grace.
"Where would you eat like this," my father asks,
passing the homemade bread, "except in Queensland?"
A lovely room. Windows give on the garden,
rose and green panes of bubble-glass enchanting
the dullest day. The sideboard mirror offers
more light. Such light, restoring, recomposing
many who dined here. Most of them are dead.


## III

"That's enough of pentameters,"
says Crab, returning to my dream.
— What shall I write, I ask. He writes,
so I won't miss his fearful joke:
 THE DIRE BELLY VARIATIONS!

Making himself a cairn of stones
he says, "This is my own rock group.
O I'm the original punk rocker
with a hatpin through my brain, my brain,
with a diamond hatpin through my brain."

— Your jokes are awful. "I know worse."
— Impossible. "Shall I rehearse
the names of those who've died from cancer?
O I'm the original merry prankster,
a diamond hatpin's all my eye.

Tell me, where are those who ate
my claws, my tender body meat?
Laurel and Hardy fans, long gone!
You cracked my hardware, ate my software.
Now I'm programmed in your brain."

IV

More and more of the great questions,
such as: what am I doing here
in gumboots and a summer nightdress
in a moonlit garden chasing sheep?

The sheep are out. It's not a dream.
I'll mend the broken fence tomorrow.
What's left of night? Enough to dream in.
What dreams will come? Who else but Crab.

I ate him sixty years ago.
Ocean of memory, transposing
feaster and feast. He beckons, wearing
seaweed clothes, with sidelong charm.

"Shall we go to a pirate movie?"
— You like the sea? "I like the bodies,
and 'Take the lady below and make
her comfortable', that's what I like.

I can't be bothered with the love scenes.
I've opened hearts. I know what's in them."
At interval he buys refreshments,
"Two seafood sticks. One without crab.

Come live with me and be my supper
where colours have no boundaries,
where every word is writ in water,
I'll put my arm around your waist.

I'll put my armour round your waist.
Shell after shell my soft self waxes.
Seek help! Sea kelp for drowning sailors.
Great questions all have wavering answers."

Ghosts crowd to hear. O my lost loves.
Waking to hard-edge sunlit colours,
sharp birdsong, lamb-bleat, I recall
myself among the moonlit sheep

questioning — what? Why should I care
how long ago my death began?
Am I a ghost dreaming I'm human
with herbs to plant, a fence to mend?

# The Magic Land of Music

I doubted from the beginning
that music was universal.
My mother was always arranging
matinees, soirees, functions
at which, in those innocent days
when even the wireless was rare,
her musical friends performed.

There was one called Irmtraud, who played
only largo and molto adagio;
any slow movement that didn't
divide beyond semiquavers
she rendered langsam und sehnsuchtsvoll
while her fidgeting rivals rolled
their eyeballs in utter boredom.

My mother sang sharp to my father's
accompaniment; my father,
whose ear was perfect, complained.
I had a particular loathing
for my teacher's favourite, Czerny.
Everybody loathed somebody
sometime, in the land of music.

I had one pupil who wished
to learn only De Camptown Ladies
and learned it, and quit for good,
and a boyfriend who told me crisply
"For Godsake don't play me Lieder"
replaced by another who wanted
Für Elise ad infinitum.

I heard the perhaps apocryphal
tale of a talented girl
with absolute pitch, growing up
in the backblocks with a deaf mother,
the piano so out of tune
that the child was riddled for life
and couldn't make sense of music.

Now I wonder what will remain
of our art in the nuclear winter.
What music will rise from the ruins?
Rodents, they say, will survive,
cockroach and scorpion flourish.
But only the wind will howl
langsam und sehnsuchtsvoll.

# 1945

Nineteen forty-five. I have been sick
all the way from Brisbane; first time in the air.
My husband's waiting in civilian clothes.
Another name now. All those burning glances
cancelled, all those raging letters burned.
And my mocking friends — "Holy MaTRIMony!"
"You've had your wings trimmed. You'll be Mother Goose."

We melt with good old-fashioned happiness
at the desolate terminal. I see the city
ending in bush, St George's on the skyline,
KEENS CURRY on the hill. We find a cafe.
"Lunch is off. Afternoon tea's not on,"
the waitress snaps, and sniffs. She knows we're strangers.
Saturday afternoon. How doth the city

sit solitary. A shuttered delicatessen
proclaims HIGH GRADE AND CONTINENTAL
 FOODSTUFFS.
What continent? Perhaps they mean the mainland.
I'm in my summer clothes. A wind breathes cold
truth in those English trees that tried to fool me
with their false fronts on a tourist office poster.
Know'st thou the land wherein the citrons bloom?

I do. Exile's the name I give that knowledge.
Even as I say How Beautiful How Charming
why do I feel that some demonic presence
hovers where too much evil has been done
near the harmless rivulet, the Georgian buildings?
Hungry, we link our lives and wait for evening.
In my husband's luggage the *Tractatus* waits

with the world that was the case already fading.


# Forty Years On

*To Peter Bennie*

I hear you are writing your memoirs,
old love. Are we all to go back
and inhabit the selves we abandoned
on Promenade Batter-My-Heart
and dance with our circle of lovers
in a strange resolution of distance?

We always turn first to the index
(speak truth!) to discover our name,
which now may be all we have left
of magical light and a body

untempered and whole. To be *there*,
and to feel the malicious delight

of naming the who-shall-be-nameless:
the White Russian who lived like an owl
undisturbed in a house of ill fame;
the curate who catechized boys
from his bathtub.
                A madrigal-mixing
of alases and hey-nonny-nonnies:

young women who flocked to your smile
fell quiet. The war was over.
Our heroes returned and reclaimed us,
and life in the suburbs began
in earnest, however deadly.
Virtue was thick on the ground.

Come unto the index all you
who hankered for life everlasting
and only got life (which is endless,
as Wittgenstein says, in the way
that our visual field has no limit).
And the inward eye, too, without limit

looks away from the shuffle of autumn
and fills with perpetual summer:
a circle, and you among us
most loved of all, discoursing
on life and art, and no one
thinking of forty years on.

# Sunset, Oyster Cove

*To the memory of Edwin Tanner*

I know better than to lie down
in sunshine in late afternoon
to drowse and wake at twilight with torturing midges
when those who know me so well
they could find me on any shore on earth
take for their breath the nightwind's: *Exile, exile.*

To all, to lovers, to friends
secure beyond falling out of love,
time brings at last their last time on earth together.
Let memory lie like sunlight
on this desolation of weeds.
    You are raked with pain, but alive, and paintings stand

    round the cave of your room; in the shadow
    of death, your death, they are binding
    your life to inviolate space.
                         For what do we grieve
if death is only an image
in the mirror of time's abyss,
the prior darkness when earth did not contain us?

How long, how late we would talk
of death, love, art, the enchanting
confusion of mortal questions. We could have talked
for a thousand years, and changed
our minds a thousand times,
like Goethe changing "For all must melt away

to nothing," after his friends
had it set in golden letters
for a scientific assembly.

                              I fear those dreams
when those I loved, now dead,
are speaking to those who died
in earlier times; they did not meet on earth

but smile, and know. They bid me:
restore, repair, remember.
Be with me here as you were, in pain but smiling,
here where the dying race
posed stiffly as grim dolls
for their last likeness, history closing round them.

As sunset paints neglected
damson and lively thistle,
and the tide returns to send the semaphore crabs
each to his burrow, flaunting
a pugilistic nipper,
affirm, "No being can dissolve to nothing."


# Resurrection

Night-coolness on glittering pasture
still, as my grandmother came
from her watch by a dying neighbour.

She sleepless, and I with my dreams
wide open to quickening day
as I fidgeted under the hairbrush:

"Her soul has taken flight."
I thought of a humanoid bird
flapping off above sounds of daybreak,

Willie Wagtail, poultry-bicker,
axe-echo, rattle of trace-chains,
to perch on God's golden throne.


— Are we doing some fowls today?
"No, today's not a day for killing,
my dear. Go and catch the butcher."


So I waved to his cart from the gate
where an elderly rooster, reprieved,
crowed up his second-last morning.


The pick of the cart! He cut
our joint; heavy carcasses swung
from the roof as he trimmed and grunted,


"So the dippy old maid has kicked it!"
My grandmother frowned rebuke.
"Our *neighbour* has *gone to heaven*."


With the rudeness permitted to one
whose wife was flighty, he barked,
"Don't give me the resurrection!


Those millions! It stands to reason
there wouldn't be space to hold them.
there simply wouldn't be room!"


I saw pig-pale bodies depending
from hooks in their jaws, and God
with a knife in bilious light


distracted: "No room! No room!"
But my grandmother, counting her change,
said, "Remember God isn't a butcher,

as time will tell."
>                    I am older
than she was then. Time has told me
less than I need to know.

If eternal life can be given
let me have it again as a child
among those whom I did not love

enough, while they lived. Let me wake,
if I wake at all, on the threshold
of day in my father's house

believing all riddles have answers
night gone  my grandmother walking
head bowed    over glittering pasture.


# Mid-Channel

*The days shall come upon you, that he will take you away*
*with hooks, and your posterity with fishhooks*
—Amos, IV, 2

Cod inert as an old boot,
tangling dance of the little shark,
perch nibble, flathead jerk —
blindfold I'd know them on my line.

Fugitive gleam on scale and fin,
lustrous eye, opalescent belly
dry and die in the undesired
element. A day will come,

matter-of-fact as knife and plate,
with death's hook in my jaw, and language
unspeakable, the line full out.
I'll tire you with my choking weight

old monster anchored in the void.
My God, you'll wonder what you've caught.
Land me in hell itself at last
I'll stab and swell your wounds with poison.

Not here, not now. Water's my kingdom
tonight, my line makes starspecks tremble.
The dinghy's decked with golden eyes
and still the cod boil round my bait.

# Pastorals

*To Desmond Cooper*

I  *Threshold*

Know that a peaceful harbour
framed by low hills, a refuge
that might be glimpsed one moment
in a happy dream, exists:
a marina spiky with masts;
salt glitter, boat-brightness rocking
in grey-green shallows, and gulls
reading in deeper sea-gleam
the text of wind and tide.

Some genius of earth
devised this generous place,
this charm of light compacting
sea, sky, the hills of Bruny,
the birds with airfilled bones,
the clouds like ghosts of sails,
into one form, one presence
whose guests we are, and welcome.
The ferry's engines throb

among water's ancient voices.
Children's and seabirds' cries
fade at the fringe of language
as the road leads gently upwards
to a gate where casuarinas
crosshatch the shining water.
The road leads on. But pause:
lift clear from time's refractions,
from the mind's reflective tricks,

this day; see its true shape.
Look how a lizard skims
from leaf-shade, and is basking
stone-still on stone, a finger-length
creature absorbing sunlight.
A crow with steel-bright eye
testing the pitch of silence
flaps to a neighbouring pine,
settles his dark voice down;

pause for a moment here.
These gums that fracture light
are home to the intricate compound
eyes of the insect kingdom,
and birds, whose eyes can read
the to-us-invisible pattern
of the polarized sky, are singing
what is real but still unnamed.
Our words and thoughts are polished

like pebbles ground in the stream
of time, but here's an enclave,
land held in arms of water,
where the plover and their young
are safe in feathery grasses
stirred by the seawind breathing
a prayer of peace and healing
in the pure, authentic speech
that earth alone can teach.


II    *A Welcome: Flowers and Fowls*

Field of the cloth of gold!
Random as stars, the dandelions
crowd in their constellations.

A day of muted brightness
but for these blazing flowers
through which, at first by ones

and twos, then all at once,
a friendly host comes running.
Two beauties walk together,

Moorish princesses, distant
from the common flock; a few
are glossed in autumn colours,

bronze, sepia, russet brown.
All gather close and turn
their sharp archaic profiles —

> You should have come with gifts
> to us of ancient lineage.
> We scratched the dust of Egypt.

> Caesar carried us north.
> We voyaged with Columbus.

I walk on, empty-handed

through taller reeds and grasses.
"O happy living things" —
as Coleridge says, the heart

must bless them, to be blessed.
And when at last I leave,
the flock, in benediction,

waits in the field of gold.
Seed of the seed of grasses
they fossick in will flourish.

Beyond the net of language
they know themselves immortal
as grassblade and grasshopper,

as the gods who fill their dishes.


III  *Mt Mangana in the Distance*

The One, the Many: with or without
capital letters they remain
or change and pass through language, thought
and those half-apprehended moments
when strands of glittering atoms twine
together in one grand design.

An early Greek philosopher called
the triangle *first-born of beauty*:
first geometric form to hold
multeity in unity.
It does philosophy no harm
to settle for such angular charm.

Sharp tenderness of early spring:
let no abstraction crop the mind.
The wind that spoke of snow is gone.
Love-vine and running postman bring
promise of paradise regained.
The house, so long at home among

those creatures here by right, prepares
its gifts of foreign fruit and flowers,
holds welcoming windows to new light.
Old songs of earthly innocence
rise up on delicate beams of bone
as earth reframes her elegant

geometry, an earth so fluent
in mathematics she composes
skin, scale, fur, feather, leaf and petal
in cusp, curve, spiral, hexagon;
and for a loving eye encloses
one prospect in three planes of vision

the casuarinas' endless outlines
rough-sketched on foreground sky and water;
two distant arms of land dividing
distant water and sky, and last
the mountain, at the heart of distance,
a triangle of softest blue.


IV   *Arcady*

Mankind's ancestral dream:
one part of earth, one place
of elemental peace.
Fields, trees, a welcoming house;
water an eye reflecting
a calm world-spanning light
on hills the hand of time
smooths to a gradual curve;
shelter, refreshment set
for birds whose song was old
when history was new;
young trees planted to grow
among the pasture grasses
the Greek heroes walked through:
man's landscape goes with him.

From blue, green, bronze, grey, muted
by cloud-shadow, the mind
turns to a deeper colour

flourishing by the house:
part of ourselves, our books,
our elegies that summer
cannot be made to stay,
part of the breath sent sobbing
after lost presences,
the red rose with its legends
of beauty and desire
speaks of the skill unearthing,
from the common briar, a form
as bright as any dream.


V  *Reflections*

Two worlds meet in the mirror
  of the quiet dam. The trees
lift stem and crown above
  their own calm images.

Rest, in the heart's dry season,
  where the green reeds stitch light
to light, where water levels
  unendingly the bright

ripple of leaf or wind-breath;
  inverts the bowl of sky
to a cup of deep enchantment,
  as if some perfect eye

saw memory and substance
  as one, and could restore
in depth, in flawless detail,
  time as it was before.

Why does the body harbour
  no memory of pain,
while a word, a name unspoken
  in the mind cuts to the bone?

When time is turned to anguish,
  lastborn of nature, rest,
where shade and water offer
  solace to all who thirst.


VI  *Autumn Rain*

Chill rain: the end of autumn.
 A day of sombre music,
a raindrop army drumming

to the plover's haunting cry.
Grief under a gold mask,
perhaps? More likely, joy

at the delicate abundance
stirring in sodden paddocks
to nourish generations

of spurred grey wings. A day
for the householder to listen
in peace to his tanks filling,

or watch the mushrooms making
themselves from almost nothing
in their chosen place, a domed

city among the pines;
but to any eye beneath them
dark suns with rays extending.

A day to think of death,
perhaps, or of children's children
inheriting the earth.

## VII  *Winter Afternoon*

A sun too mild to challenge
frost in the shady hollows
honours this afternoon
with light so sharp the gulls
a mile away flash silver.

Cold underfoot, how cold
the touch of air on hand
and face in lengthening shadows
by the dam's hoof-churned rim.
Explicit darkness stamps

and snorts. Two young bulls wheel
away, return and circle
like boys at play exploding
with aimless energy,
then stand stock-still, exhaling

a sour-sweet mash of grasses.
Clear light glosses their blackness:
taut flank, keel-curving breast,
bold eyeball, glistening muzzle
plumed with the warmth of breath.

No word that makes us mortal
touches their strength, or glints
on their serene horizon:
this winter's day, this field
where earth has set their table.

## VIII  *Sea Eagle*

Dusk, early springtime. Light's a tender
grey monotone, and silver-cold
water's a mirror where the slender
grasses in stony shallows hold
their shadows still. Twilight uncovers
old nightfall sorrows: friends and lovers
long lost, once beautiful. The hills
of Bruny darken. Darkness fills
thin ribs of water as the wading
herons stab at the edge of night.
Wingbeats: from a bare branch the white-
breasted sea eagle soars in fading
cloudlight. A late gleam from the west
catches him riding on a crest

of air to his untroubled gleaming
eminence. He turns and drifts,
his mile of quiet water seeming
a wingspan wide. How the heart lifts
from old hesperian sadness, follows
him homeward through the shadowy hollows
between the hills, accepting all:
the lordly hunter and the small
creatures who tremble at his rising.
Night voices wake as night comes on
and conjure when the last light's gone
the always known, always surprising
flight of the mind that soars to share
his pathway in cold shires of air.

## IX  *Carapace*

Hold in the hollow of your palm
this carapace so delicate
one breath would send it spinning down,
yet strong enough to bear the stress
of ebb, flow, metamorphosis
from skin to shell.
                    Seasons have scoured
this beautiful abandoned house
from which are gone eyes, sinews, all
taken-for-granted gifts.
                    I hold
in my unhoused continuing self
the memory that is wisdom's price
for what survives and grows beneath
old skies, old stars.
                    Fresh mornings rim
the carapace of night with gold.
The sandgrains shine, the rockpools brim
with tides that bring and bear away
new healing images of day.

from *The Present Tense* (1995)

# The Present Tense

*I.M. Vincent Buckley*

"What does it mean to move
out of the present tense?"
I asked you in a dream
not long after your death.
You said, "We live two lives.
One in the world, and one
in what others write about us."
In the dream it was towards evening.

> As many suns in the galaxy
> as nerve cells in the brain.
> My skull's a dome of darkness,
> the only room of my own
> I'll have this side of death.

Today's the feast of Corpus Christi.
*Honey out of the rock.* The sun
after a moment's elevation
is veiled in a Bridgewater Jerry.
Seagulls head for the tip. My blackbird
takes his life in his throat. The sparrows
come close for crumbs. Is this a world
containing in itself all hunger?

Pain's your continuing absence from the world
among other matters.
                    "Love is not a feeling.
     Why is pain not put to the test like love?
      If it were true pain, would it go away?"
Who said such things? Saint Ludwig of Vienna.
That thinker should have used the Queensland *but*.
Love's not a feeling, but. Real pain is not
put to the test, but. Doesn't sound so pompous.

A difficult man, one much in need of friendship.
A genius. Didn't like women, but.
Thank God you did. It was beatitude
to talk shop to a man who plainly liked me.
You'd met the doctor who nursed Wittgenstein.

> The bells of Holy Trinity
> call the living. Foursquare, massive,
> crowned with spirelets, Blackburn's tower
> is silhouetted on rolling mist.
> Great bells have jostling overtones
> containing, Leonardo thought,
> the timbre of all human voices.
> Where's yours? The crescent honeyeater
> offers a senseless answer: EGYPT.

This north-east facing cottage suits
one with four-in-the-morning horrors.
I'm always up to see the sunrise,
know where the sun is when it's cloudy.

One of my children built Stonehenge in balsa
as it was when it was new, in perfect scale.
On the first night we ever ate together
he showed you how the stones were oriented,
and where the sun rose on midsummer morning.
"There was human sacrifice," he said with relish.

Tired after our gentle-hearted
walk by the billabong, you went
homeward by car, and when we parted
I walked back slowly, thinking over
our discourse, with the firm intent
of fixing in my head forever,

as in a painting, the spring light
of happiness on children chasing
their happy dogs, the Sunday-bright
families and the brilliant blue
parrots feeding in grass; clouds racing
shadows fleeting as thought. I drew

near to your house. A man was sitting
on a low garden wall, outlined
in evening light, his body fitting
itself to age and pain. He heard
my footstep, rose and smiled. We twined
arms, and walked on without a word.


# Autumn

*To the memory of Vincent Buckley*

Once in Melbourne, billeted
in a lecturer's room at Ormond,
I answered the phone expecting
a call from you, and breathed,
con amore, Irish Darling.
A startled professor replied
"I seem to have got the wrong room."

An earlier winter night
in Hobart: my children show you
their treasures, shells, fossils, a scale
model of Stonehenge in balsa.
One gives you a lecture on Druids
while I get the dinner, find pencils,
check schoolbags, rehearse the homework.

I Mother, you in the haze
of your academic glory,
younger than I, and sadder
than I have ever been,
we talk when the house is quiet.
I remember your saying, "Happiness
precludes the greatest joy."

Nearly thirty years on I am sitting
playing Scrabble with your young daughters.
One gives me a lecture on guineapigs
while your wife is getting the dinner.
Our last day on earth together.
Grania waits through the game
to put down her one word: Ireland.

Some say that primates evolved
concurrently with fruit trees;
we passed them on, they gave us
our colour vision, our taste for sweetness.
What gave us our salty rapture then
at a cry from the stage: It is no matter now
who lives or who dies.

What's metaphor to me,
or nature playing at theatre.
Let autumn repeating its moral office
of ripeness, let its adorning
be blown away, away.
Things pile up, a heap of crutches:
the must-be-done. Props for the living.

Rake, pruning shears, a fire
of dry leaves gilded with death.
"More and more of the immortals
were dying," you wrote. I was charmed
by your presence in the world
to distraction. The day is far spent,
Irish Darling. It's mortals who die.


# Midwinter Rainbow

*I.M. Vincent Buckley*

The immortal Signified
has deconstructed light.
Adonai Elohim,
I-am-that-I-am,
ineffable by name
and nature, hangs his sign
aloft for all to read.
How to deduce the rules
of his chromatic game?
Newton figured a path
for sunlight's deviation.
Save us from Newton's sleep,
said visionary Blake.
Read the scriptures and weep:
save us from one who makes
promises, promises
to Noah, that old soak,
and then, nine chapters on,
sits eating veal and cakes
prepared by Abraham's wife
before he torches Sodom,
just and unjust together.

I will be when and where
I will be, saith the Lord.
God, what a character!
Where could he set the rainbow
in that anterior age
when there was none to see it?

You laughed once when I told you
the luminous space between
inner and outer rainbows
is called Alexander's Band.

Wrap me in rags of time.
You are gone to the treasures
of darkness. I remain.
Some ancient presence writes
a soft-edged covenant
beyond interpretation
on the midwinter sky.


# Night Thoughts

"Hell is for those who doubt that hell exists."
One of the elohim with whom I fight
from 4 a.m. to cockcrow, told me this.
He hit me in the thigh for emphasis.
Is it a dream? If so, the dream persists.

I meet him always at the edge of night.
He knows me, but he'll never give his name.
Why should you know, he says. I have to guess
whether he comes to punish or to bless.
I thought once he was death, but at first light

he goes, and I get up. Things are the same
as usual. The sounds of day begin:
the kettle and the news; so it's not death
who comes in the small hours to cramp my breath.
Sleep is extinguished like a candle flame.

Longing for peace I wrestle, try to pin
the adversary down. Tell me your name.
Tell me, did language lapse when mankind fell?
Tell me, is "He descended into hell"
a metaphor? The literal truth? Where in

this universe could hell be? He persists:
"Hell is for those who doubt that hell exists."


## To Music

You of the Minute Waltz and the Four Seasons,
you of the earthen flute and grand piano,
you with your immortal numbers:
the Nine, the Thirty-two, the Forty-eight;
you of the infant trying out the pitch
of its few syllables, you of the birds,
of the first cuckoo in spring, the lark ascending
to carve its empire in a thousand notes;
you of Gaudeamus and Miserere,
music, fitting yourself to any language,
at home with love and death and revolution.
Music, made of the very air we breathe,
with us from everlasting, always new,
in throats, in guts, in horsehair and wooden bellies.
Sleeping for centuries in forgotten scores,
hiding in crumhorn, shawm, theorbo, sackbut,

rattling in the tambourine, rejoicing
at the horse and his rider flung into the sea,
silent by Babel's streams, hung on the willows,
loud in national anthems, marching with bagpipes,
jogging in headphones, waiting in lifts and buses,
lurking in telephones, raging in discos
everywhere
                  nowhere without a human ear.


# Herongate

*To Graeme Hetherington*

I dream I am opening the door
of Herongate lost in the fire,
gone into the world of light
in one way or another, if dreams
are as real as anything else.

In the dream the house is intact,
a world without metaphor, standing
foursquare, with its ramshackle shed
and its tanks and wreathing geraniums.
So all is well, after all,

until I look down at my hand,
at my fingers turning the key:
my bones are as white as a long-bleached shell,
as smooth, as beautiful.
I have died. It was I who died

and have come in my dream to this door,
a skeleton in a summer dress,
whose dream was fire, whose language

must manage without any tongue
of fire, or anything else.

And what will my fingers write
without sinew or flesh, though the bones
by some strange gravitational force
that seems to be partial to dactyls
are turning my key in the lock.

O my bird-haunted shack in the dunes!
A nest that I shaped to myself.
There are streets I can't cross for the ghosts,
but in Paradise nothing can happen.
Alone, I invested in silence,

except for the resident possums.
I hope they escaped from the fire.
This hope marks the edge of my dream
as I wake in the city, alive.
Far off, a faint bloom in the marshes

is announcing a change of season,
and perhaps an invisible presence
that does not startle the herons
cries out by the desolate tankstands
to purge its grief, is waiting

like a satyr straight out of Isaiah
with the cormorant and the bittern
possessing the stones of emptiness
until I return, to tell me
my days will not be prolonged.

# Wittgenstein's Shoebox

Tell me, ye powers that dwell below,
how did this shoebox come to be
on a stall in Salamanca market?

Are they philosophers approaching?
No, clergymen. I needn't worry.
Fifty cents, and it's mine for ever.

The box is crammed with paper slips:
mixed-up observations, thoughts
on the origins of human language.

>Think of a language where each word
>is used and understood once only.
>Leaf-drift of useless syllables!

>If a cane toad could be taught to speak
>how could we know if it were lying?
>Think of the neural infrastructure.

Here's the man himself. He wants his box back.
"Ludwig —." He scowls. "Herr Wittgenstein,
has the verb *to dream* a present tense?"

I tell him, "Once I saw a raven
eating chips from a paper bag
on a high branch of this very plane tree.

*Corvus tasmanicus*. Believe me."
He doesn't and the paper strips
fly up and deck the tree with leaves.

I wake, as always, with my problems
unsolved. It's true about the raven.
I can bring you a living witness.


# Songs of Eve II

*To James Penberthy*

I

Adam came in from his bird-watching,
flopped on the grass, said "Where's my dinner?"
Get it yourself, I said, there's plenty
of everything, just go and pick it.
"What's that you're reading," he said. I said
I've bought this set, the Book of Knowledge.
It will help me to get ahead.
Such a nice salesman. Try this apple.

II

What of that other woman
the scriptures do not name?
Cain's wife, who bore him children
could not be held to blame
for my fault, or Adam's fault,
or any fault in Cain.
So, when she bears her children,
why should she suffer pain?

III

>Look how I tamed
>  the unicorn
>    who laid in my lap
>      his fearful horn
>        and now adores me
>          says he's my slave
>            and buys me a Porsche
>             and a microwave
>              and a washing machine
>               and a fan-forced oven
>                and all the symphonies
>                 of Beethoven
>                  on compact disc
>                   and a great TV
>                    and a queensized waterbed
>                     just for me.

## A Piece of Ivory

I would grieve over fallen finches,
drowned frogs, an occasional duckling
that did not live to be eaten,
but this was beyond me.
                        At bedtime
my father said "You remember
the circus you saw at Enoggera?
Well, one of the elephants went mad
and killed a keeper who used to torment it."

"And serve him right," my grandmother said.

My father continued "It had to be shot.
They made the other elephants dig it a grave
in the paddock, and help to bury it."

I saw them in wrinkled twilight
swaying with spades in their trunks,
chained one to another, crying
and digging a grave for their friend.

Next morning, unroofing the graves
of Finch, Frog, Duck, I ran howling
at what gave shine to the world
then took it away forever.

I remember my grandmother's comfort,
my being allowed to play
with her particular treasure:
an enamelled Indian casket
full of handcarved ivory elephants,
diminishing, the smallest
the size of a grain of wheat.
But carved. The artist cared.

# Later Texts

I

She sits in the park, wishing she'd never written
about that dowdy housewife and her brood.
Better, the Memoirs of a Mad Sex-Kitten,
or a high-minded Ode to Motherhood
in common metre with a grand doxology.
"They have eaten me alive." Did she write that?
The sonnet nestles in a new anthology
safe in its basket as a favoured cat.

She sits a while in flickering light rehearsing
the family's birthdays. "Stop, you bloody fool!"
A young house-father with a pram is cursing
a child who's pushed another in the pool.
She helps him calm them. "Eating you alive?
Look at me. I've lived through it. You'll survive."

II

She practises a fugue for pure enjoyment,
the graceful C sharp major from Book One.
Friends call. "Still at your classical employment?"
She plays it through for them. The setting sun
blazes on a brass owl, a grandchild's present.
Owls are not passerines. The claws are wrong.
They sit with drinks. She shows them an unpleasant
poison-pen letter. "Where does this belong?"

"Why not donate it to a library?
Give the anonymous pest one taste of fame.
Make work for a detective PhD."
They talk of absent friends, and what became
of children (middle-aged now), and the past.
Be wise, my sorrow. Evening falls at last.

III

*Eloisa to Abelard*

Believe me, here behind the veil all's well.
Less work, more time for reading. Writing, too.
Eventually one leaves Heartbreak Hotel.
So, how are things? I sometimes think of you,
Sweetheart, and now and then I wonder what
Topics you lecture on. Still keen on Bede?
Historia Calamitatum's not
Everyone's title. Still, it's a good read.
Expect you'll sell a few. I hope to put
Down a few thoughts in writing. About us.
I hear you're up for heresy. Appeal
To Rome, why don't you? Bernard needs the boot,
Or swatting with De Intellectibus.
Rock on, old love. I know just how you feel.

# The Owl and the Pussycat Baudelaire Rock

You longed for night and the night is coming,
    the rays of the daystar fade and die,
the nightwind rises, the tide is waiting,
    and the years that are gone lean down from the sky.
    Baby my baby, I'll love you forever,
      when your head's burned out and your light's all gone,
    my eyes will find you in stony darkness.
    Baby my baby the night comes on.

Rock on, rock on till we reach that country
    where all is harmony and delight,
fragrance of amber, fathomless mirrors
    reflecting the gold and hyacinth light.
    Baby my baby I'll love you forever,
      when your brain's ground out and your dreams are gone
    I'll hunt you out through seas of darkness.
    Baby my baby the night comes on.

Rock on, rock on, my songs enfold you,
    the moon slides down and the water's wild,
the snowpeaks gleam on the far horizon,
    the sun will rise like a golden child.
    You asked for night and look it is falling
    your peace is here, your sorrow is gone,
    lie at my side in the rocking darkness.
    Baby my baby, the night comes on.

# A Selection of Uncollected Poems, 1944–1994

# The Rite of Spring

The Jew Stravinsky bidden to the feast
turns host, invites the virgins with bassoons.
The triple hammers pleading for the wise
shatter our flutes, the foolish Sibyl cries:
Lanterns in spring are silly poets' lies.

They said: the cuckoo singing in the leaves
is a false cuckoo, all the birds are come
to Lycia. Above the twisted spears
singing they flew to follow sleep and death
who bore the body of Sarpedon home.

Europa's husband walking to the bank
heard the false cuckoo, and its hollow song
recalled his mistress, though the vanished night
could offer him no trusted antidote
nor drain the cunning poison from delight.

The music done, in silence time recalls
and shapes the moment, lending him relief.
The unassuming river of his blood
flows without torment, passing through the streets
of troubled cities broken by its flood.

*Gwendoline Foster*   (1949)

# Space Poem

We stopped at a large asteroid
  during our transgalactic run.
The crew, all bored and bloody-minded,
  got off determined for some fun.

Some F-type alienoids were hanging
  from rocks by their pink sucker-pads.
They soon let go. Those who resisted
  took a fair beating from my lads.

Then from the cliff above a shower
  of pebbles struck the ground like hail –
an M-type on a ledge stood swinging
  a great stone in his functional tail.

He killed a man before I got him
  in the disintegrator ray.
The crew retreated to the airlock.
  The F-types screamed and climbed away.

I've called the medic-bank in Theta
  on my molecular stenophone.
We must have got a bug, or virus.
  The crew are sickening one by one.

The specimen we caged is thriving,
  watching me as I close this file.
My God, I'd swear the thing was smiling
  if I thought things like that could smile.

*T.F. Kline*   (1969)

# Frog Prince

The honeymoon went swimmingly.
She kissed him, glad that his touch was
cooler than cool. He asked the right
questions in the right tone of voice.
They danced all night beside the pool.

In bed she found him playfully
absurd. A year passed. Childless still,
she made a quilt embroidered with
her parents' coat of arms. He grew
stouter, suffered from warts, drank more.

Somehow the landscape changed in scale.
He strolled among the places where
water grew foul. A dripping fringe
of moss grew from the eaves. He swiped
at flies, and caught them on the wing.

One night something appalling flopped
on top of her. Her parents came
next day to visit, and found all
the ceilings weeping, their girl raped,
her mouth stuffed with a golden ball.

*T.F. Kline*   (1970)

# Emporium

Young Lady, what can I do for you?
Yes, of course, you want a lover.
We have this unrepeatable offer:
this beautiful model with floating hair.
Just look at the eyes! Of course it's tricky
to handle, the only one of its kind.
Think how your friends will envy you.

My dear young lady, back already?
So the model got out of control in the dark?
And the words he used when he chose to speak
didn't seem to suit your lovely home?
And your parents insist on trading him in?

Well, may I suggest our regular number,
our knitting-book type, as cool and smooth
as his cigarette, in Alpine drag,
germ-free, complete with sag-proof smile.

Good morning, Madam, yes I can guess,
you've settled down and you'd like a child.
They come in all kinds, you can take your pick.
This one won't give you a moment's worry:
all-girl, all-boy, yes, one of each,
good on their potties, pretty and clean,
obedient, socially well-adjusted.
What else could Madam possibly want?

Good morning, good morning, of course I remember.
If Madam was so dissatisfied
why did she not say so at the time?
Diseases, nightmares, obscure neuroses? —
Dear lady, those models were factory-clean
and we couldn't possibly trade them in.

But down in the basement we happen to have
that very old model with flashing eyes
(and hair still good!) . . . If Madam cares
to take it away she might possibly find
a part that could be used to fill
that gaping hole in Madam's heart.

*T.F. Kline*   (1975)


# Last Meeting

Shadows grazing eastward melt
from their vast sun-driven flocks
into consubstantial dusk.
A snow wind flosses the bleak rocks,

strips from the gums their rags of bark,
and spins the coil of winter tight
round our last meeting as we walk
the littoral zone of day and night,

light's turncoat margin: rocks and trees
dissolve in nightfall-eddying waters;
tumbling whorls of cloud disclose
the cold eyes of the sea-god's daughters.

We tread the wrack of grass that once
a silver-bearded congregation
whispered about our foolish love.
Your voice in calm annunciation

from the dry eminence of thought
rings with astringent melancholy:
"Could hope recall, or wish prolong
the vanished violence of folly?

Minute by minute summer died;
time's horny skeletons have built
this reef on which our love lies wrecked.
Our hearts drown in their cardinal guilt."

*The world*, said Ludwig Wittgenstein,
*is everything that is the case.*
— The warmth of human lips and thighs;
the lifeless cold of outer space;

this windy darkness; Scorpio
above, a watercourse of light;
the piercing absence of one face
withdrawn for ever from my sight.

(1957)


# The Double Image

*To Rex Hobcroft*

We rest here, where no hours
but the sun's time need be kept.
Fossils speak from the rocks
of a time when this land slept
as ocean's floor. The creek
runs clear in its tumbled bed.

Gentle, and light of heart,
your twins kneel by a pool
stirring the water-creatures;
they laugh, as water reshapes
at each other's wavering features.
Their double image shines
in water, and above:
as if air had the power
of water to reflect,
or earth itself could speak
some loved syllables twice;
they wear with double grace
marks of your singleness
in gesture, form and face.

No word can snatch or hold
those moments when we wake
alive from the sleep of time.
But heart remembers, lives
on nothing, if need be,
until it wakes again
tasting joy it cannot name.
I seize this joy and hear
live water's countless voices
and singing lips of flame
where the sun burns, and bless
your children kneeling above
their shivering images:
with water, rock and light
caught in the pulse of *now*.

Winter floods will possess
this place, darkness this day.
Changing water will wear
inconstant rock away.

The shape, but not the life
of the vanished moment stays:
a fossil firm in rock.
Until visions wake once more
to stir life with the shock
of life, I wait, and praise
the grace that children bear
as they play in the clear water,
gentle and light of heart.

(1963)


# Hyacinth

My sisters drowsed among the flowers
drunk with longing, drunk with love,
in their familiar mental moonlight,
dreaming fulfilment, fingers tearing
hymens of unopened buds.

The God came in his car
daily, snatched me away.
My sisters waited, silenced
by his appalling wealth.
Their pale flesh sickened him.
He scorned their gaping rapture.
We left them fluttering
hysterical white hands.

Life had no images
but those fixed in his eye.
We burned along the highways
in his outlandish car.

Earth, a pastoral dream;
sea, membranes of colour.
Far off, the tarnished cities
glittered with abstract light.
Somehow our bodies solved
all physical equations,
keeping his pulsebeat hours.

Today I took the wheel
drunk with violence, drunk with love.
Down, down through private horror
the bright disc spun towards me
matter and colour fused
the world in one explosion.

My head lolls on its stalk.
My sisters kneel beside me
stroking my hair and screaming
at the darkness on their fingers.

(1973)

# In Memoriam Sela Trau

*I learned both what is secret and what is manifest,*
*for wisdom, the fashioner of all things, taught me.*

Your word was always: *Peace*. Peace of the spirit,
a calm and luminous landscape of the soul
where peace was the clear atmosphere you breathed.

In this grim century of dispossession
you gave us your supreme possession, music.
Sela: your very name is linked with music,

as in the Psalms: a rest, an interlude,
a pause, without which music can't exist.
When the vibrations died, you'd hold your bow

briefly in utter stillness, so we listened
to that pure silence from which music grows.
Mother, musician, teacher, virtuoso

in the true sense of the word, from *virtus*,
strength, bravery, courage, virtue, excellence.
One of your pupils said that what she owed you

could never be repaid, except with life,
a life that showed what never could be spoken,
as music shows, if we have ears to hear it,

a wealth of life transcending speech and silence.
You spoke sometimes of all things linked together,
from starry space to flowers and all earth's creatures,

all one, both visible and invisible.
That perfect health and perfect peace might flourish
seemed possible to you, O pure of heart

to whom the tree of wisdom gave its shelter
in your long life. You counted as a blessing
that time you could not play your instrument

because of injury. "A time to think
in quietness," you said, "about those things
I've had no time to think of."

We think of you under the aspect of eternity
in springtime, when the earth is rich with blossom.
Your vision lights us. Sela, rest in peace.

(1991)


## Late Works

Time to think of your Late Works
in the pure daylit atmosphere
of mystical acceptance, freedom
from old monsters, etcetera.

Time to be calmly transcendental
and abstract, time to set the stakes
so high no one will bet on you,
fill any form with stuff that breaks

the form so everything pours out
in a Great Fugue no one can play.
All those you wanted to impress
are dead or sick or pretty crazy

and those you know will understand it
are not yet born. Nurse, I need paper.
No, not that kind, you idiot girl,
the kind you write on. Get me Matron,

Matron I need a fountain pen.
If you have any wits about you
they're PhDs requesting access
to things you can't remember writing

to people you don't now remember.
Time to make light of time. Forget it.
Look through it. Write those late great works.
What was it that you asked the nurse for?

No matter now. You have your life
before you, you're a child enjoying
your *self*, the unity of contrasts.
Whose hand is it that holds your pen?